What's Wrong with Economics?

Benjamin Ward

What's Wrong with Economics?

Macmillan

First published in the United States 1972
First published in the United Kingdom 1972

Published by
THE MACMILLAN PRESS LTD
London and Basingstoke
Associated companies in New York Toronto Dublin Melbourne Johannesburg and Madras

SBN 333 14613 1

Printed in Great Britain by
BIDDLES LTD
Guildford, Surrey

Acknowledgments

No doubt everyone named on this page disagrees with at least one of the major arguments of this book. Nevertheless, each of them has had a significant effect on the final product, and many of them have diverted me from substantial error. The comments of Jean Bénard, Martin Bronfenbrenner, Gregory Grossman, Ernest Nadel, Thomas Rothenberg, and Hal Varian on an earlier draft, and discussions with these people as well as with Douglas Dowd, Sherman Krupp, Ganshyam Mehta, Hanna Pitkin, Roy Radner, Richard Roehl, Ronald Schwartz, Donald Wittman, Bernard Saffran, Sidney Winter, and some discussants of a lecture given at the University of California, Davis, three years ago, are remembered with special gratitude. Had Robert Dorfman and M. M. Knight not been my teachers at Berkeley this book would probably have not been written, for they forced their students to focus on fundamentals. Members of a seminar held last winter quarter at Berkeley contributed substantially to the clarification of ideas. Eileen Grampp, Selma Gluck, and Phyllis Dexter provided most competent administrative and clerical assistance. Thanks again.

Contents

Part V Values and Deeds

Part I

Neoclassical Economics

Economics as a Science

The easiest way to answer the title question to this book would seem to be to make a list. The list of things wrong with economics would contain all those problems, from poverty and inflation to alienation and frustration, that economics has plainly not yet solved. But though this approach is taken from time to time these days, it is hardly fair to the economics profession. One does not condemn physicists for not having solved the problem of generating a perpetual-motion machine, and it is by no means inconceivable that there are social and economic problems too that are unsolvable in principle. One does not even criticize physicists for being unable to agree among themselves on many questions of fact and theory, for this is taken as a sign that physics is a lively and active science whose practitioners are seeking the truth in difficult areas. One *does* sometimes criticize physicists for helping develop basic ideas of use to the designers of weaponry, but most critics become quite selective at this point; few would condemn all physicists throughout the world who have engaged in research of potential military value. Clearly a fairly subtle criterion of judgment is needed in making out a what's-wrong-with-science-X list.

Quite a number of critical comments about economics occur in this book, and some of them are rather fundamental. They could of course be lined up in a list in the concluding chapter, but that has not been done. A list would be useful if the various items on the list were separable so that one person could start work, say, on item 3, and another on item 17. But by and large the things wrong with economics are mutually inseparable, part of a general pattern, so that in a sense everything on the list has to be changed before anything on it can be changed. Some other approach is called for.

The approach taken here is to break up the title question into a series of questions which serve to lead the discussion in the desired directions. For example the first question, the topic of this chapter, asks: Is economics a science? The answer is given within a framework which puts emphasis on sciences as social systems, that is, on the attitudes and interactions among practitioners of a given science. The approach was developed by Thomas Kuhn and applied by him to the history of natural science.[1] Here and in Chapter 2 we will be concerned with what Kuhn calls a normal science, which means among other things that over the relevant time-period scientists are sufficiently confident of the fundamentals of their subject that there is little methodological discussion. Economics seems to pass this particular test very well.

The next question is: *Should* economics (or the social sciences generally) look like the natural sciences? In

Chapters 2 and 3 this question is considered within a somewhat modified Kuhnian framework, taking account of Kuhn's notion of scientific revolution. Economics appears to possess some rather peculiar features for a science, in particular an ideology and a special kind of shortsightedness. This same question is also under discussion in Part II, where the consequences of the existence of two competing sciences dealing with more or less the same subject are considered.

Part II also begins discussion of the question that occupies the rest of the book, namely: Are there alternatives to the current structure and conceptual bases of economics? The one-sentence answer to this question is: Yes, several fields, such as language philosophy, personality psychology, situation ethics, and legal theory, provide the basis for a coherent alternative conceptual basis for economics, one that not only expands the discipline so that it can at least discuss relevant issues now swept under the table, but even holds out promise of productivity in the scientific sense. The last three parts of this book are devoted to sketching in the arguments in favor of this claim. An attempt is made to keep contrasts between neoclassical economics and these alternative approaches to the foreground. For reasons that will become apparent, Marxism is given much more limited discussion.

Kuhn's Tests

Kuhn suggests that the most useful way to look at a science is as a special kind of social system. The principal figures in this social system are the researchers, the people who do the developing of the science for their generation. When a science exists and is developing normally, it will, Kuhn predicts, be able to pass the following six tests:

1 The researchers, though they are widely scattered over universities and research institutes around the country or even the world, form a sort of invisible college, based on common interests, shared commitments, and frequent interaction.

2 Colleagues, members of a particular invisible college, are concerned to solve problems about the behavior of nature, and

3 The problems on which they typically work are problems of detail. An individual researcher is working at any one point in time on some relatively minor aspects of the science. He may be trying to improve somewhat the accuracy with which the value of some constant is known, or he may be trying to modify some portion of the theory to make it fit a new range of data. He will definitely *not* be seriously engaged in answering the question, "What's wrong with science X?"

4 Members of the invisible college are in general agreement as to what the main problems are that are suitable for research, and they are also agreed as to the general form that a solution should take. These agreements are a product of the similar training the scientists have received, the common body of theory, established fact, and laboratory procedure that they know. Of course there are many disagreements among scientists as well. But these tend to be limited by the vast lore they have in common. There may be several proposed solutions to a particular problem and disagreement as to which one is correct. But this is true only in a relatively modest number of places in the science, and even in such cases there will be pretty good agreement as to what sort of research in principle would resolve the disagreement. Indeed, this process of resolving disagreements within a broader framework of general agreement is the normal process of development of a science.

5 Only the judgment of colleagues is accepted as relevant in defining problems and solutions. If religious or political

authorities who are not trained for membership in the invisible college interfere in its operation or are accepted in practice as authorities higher than the college itself, normal science does not take place.

6 The system of problems of the science is self-sustaining; achieving accepted solutions in several areas does not reduce the number of unsolved problems of interest to colleagues. Without inquiring as to why this might be true, we may simply note Kuhn's example of a part of a science, geometric optics, that disappeared from science because it simply ran out of interesting problems.

Economics as a Social System

These six tests by no means exhaust Kuhn's theory of normal science, and other aspects of the theory will be considered in later chapters. But the tests themselves suffice as a sort of outline of important properties ascribable at least to many natural sciences. We will use them now as a basis for a somewhat casual characterization of economics as a social system.

There is nowhere a list of neoclassical economist-scientists, and the criteria by which such a list might be made would hardly provide definitive judgments in every case. For example, in a given year about four thousand authors publish articles which are noted in the standard economics index.[2] Quite a number of these authors are producing works which do not really make use of the standard skills of economists, and many researchers do not publish every year, so this suggests that the upper-limit estimate of economists who identify with the research effort will be in the thousands, though not in the tens of thousands. A lower-limit estimate might be found by simply including most of the economists located in research-oriented universities, and then adding some fraction to take account of the scattering of appropriate economists in other schools and in government. The rationale behind this figure, which would perhaps run to four or five hundred names, is that it is these economists who interact with one another sufficiently to assure full awareness of participation in the joint social venture. Just to complete this brief numbers game, around fifty to a hundred young men and two or three women enter the professional job market each year with qualifications and promise entitling them to a reasonable crack at employment in a research-oriented institution.

What makes the invisible college of economists? First and most important is the training program, for which the Ph.D. curriculum is the central ingredient. There are some common elements in these programs, to which all students are subjected, whether in the United States or the United Kingdom, or even the Soviet Union.[3] There is a modest preparation in mathematics and statistics, a general acquaintance with price theory and macroeconomics, and some historical-institutional-policy information on the functioning of at least one economy, usually the United States. These topics are learned from textbooks and "classic" papers, for which there is a great deal of overlap among curricula. Second, there is the contact with colleagues, which serves to reinforce the traditions and lore which is generally accepted. And third, there is the research itself, governed by the informal rules of the profession, whose successful accomplishment is the principal badge of honor of the scientist. Research offers continuing opportunities for personal contact, with frequent conferences and national committee work providing the basic vehicle, supplemented on almost every occasion by the telephone. Patterns of social life differ from one institution and economist to another, but probably most research economists share a substantial proportion of their recreational socializing with other economists. These activities also bring into the invisible college a number of economists who are not regular contributors to research, thus increasing substantially beyond the lower-limit figure the number of economists who identify with the scientific endeavor.

Though economics is an invisible college, it is also, like other sciences, a hierarchy, a pecking order of status and influence. The three main dimensions on which status rankings are based are institutions, fields, and individual accomplishment. Status rankings of economics departments have become institutionalized in the United States, and in the case of economics there seems to be rather general agreement among economists that the ranking based on the Cartter Report is "correct," at least in its upper reaches.[4] The ability to get general agreement on such rankings is one of the hallmarks of a science, an indicator that there is underlying agreement among practitioners as to what constitutes good-quality research.

Determination of the status accorded the various branches of the discipline is a more subtle process; such rankings are not formally attempted, and any attempt to offer such a ranking is bound to be controversial. But let us give it a try. The subfields of economics, of which there are perhaps a dozen, serve as identifying labels for practitioners in the job market. They also define the scope of fields as taught in basic courses in most economics departments, and via the textbooks, serve as the organizing force around which knowledge in the field is categorized. There are certain things one expects a practitioner of labor economics to understand that economists in general will not be expected to know, and this semispecialization is a vital part of the means by which the science is developed while maintaining a functioning invisible college.

Roughly speaking, the division of economics into the following dozen fields is supported by the ways in which formal teaching is divided into textbooks and courses in most economics departments:

A Microtheory, macrotheory, econometrics
B International trade, money and banking, public finance
C Industrial organization, labor, economic history
D Economic development, history of economic thought, comparative economic systems

For purposes of status rankings these fields are divided into four classes. Essentially the idea is that the highest status fields, those in Class A, define the nature of acceptable research problems in economics and the appropriate procedures to use in attempting to solve them. The remaining fields are classified in terms of the extent to which practitioners actually make use of the Class A framework of problems and procedures in their research. The Class D fields, for example, require a good deal of research borrowing from outside economics and contain a relatively large number of practitioners who are not well versed in the Class A topics. Some of the Class C fields are occasionally referred to as the "slum fields" of economics; the Class D fields face even more serious problems, as is perhaps reflected in their propensity to use the word "economic" even in their customary titles.

Finally, and ultimately the most important, is the ranking of individuals. As in the case of the other factors, agreement on individual status as a contributor to the science is most nearly consensual near the top of the list, because there practitioners are being judged by the most nearly consensual standards. Leaders in the field use conventional procedures in trying to solve conventional problems. Within this conventional framework, skill and ingenuity can be measured with fair accuracy. Of course an individual's status can transcend (or fall below) that of his field and his institution. The highest-status individuals have a good deal of influence on economics by virtue of the fact that among other things, they generally are both among the most prolific and the most widely read economists. But it is an influence within the conventional framework, attaching as much to his role as a professional leader as to his person. Unconventional remarks or works may well be ignored.

Despite all this emphasis on consensus, disagreements abound in economics. Perhaps the best-known controversy over the last few years is that between the monetarists and Keynesians over the relative power of monetary and fiscal policy in controlling the level of economic activity. Almost every field has comparable controversies, with qualified experts lined up on both sides of each question. But the important point is that these disagreements occur within a framework of general agreement. Keynesians and monetarists generally agree as to the nature of their disagreement and the kinds of tests that are likely to help resolve the controversy. The very nature of these disagreements implies that a way has already been found to prescribe the procedures for resolving the conflict among members of the scientific community that are generally acceptable to that community. Such disagreement within agreement lies at the heart of the process of normal development of a science.

To the layman nothing is more obvious than that economics journals are exclusively concerned with problems of detail. Nevertheless economics does differ in this respect from such a hard science as physics. If a physicist writes a book, it is almost certainly either a textbook or a handbook—or it is a personal statement of the what-physics-means-to-me sort. Serious physics appears as papers in professional journals. In recent years this has come much closer to being the truth in economics than it was, say, thirty years ago. But it is still true that some people who seem to be generally regarded as economists convey their fundamental thoughts primarily in books rather than in detailed research papers.[5] Again, the incidence of such books tends to be higher the lower the status of the relevant field.

Economics has acquired a hard core of quite esoteric knowledge which serves to separate sharply the solid, mainline practitioner from others. This core is now based on the formalization of theory and method by means of mathematics. The advent of the large scale computer has made it possible to integrate the theory with procedures for testing hypotheses based on numerical data that, in its sophistication, seems to rival the hardest parts of physics. There are probably no more than a hundred economists who have been making important contributions to this part of the field, developing the basic ideas of mathematical economics and econometrics. They are the science's élite. For practitioners within this area of economics there can be no appeal other than to their peers in the field; no one else knows what they are talking about when they are talking the language of their science.

Except for the history of economic thought all the fields of economics have been quite astonishingly self-sustaining. There are perhaps ten times the practitioners of economics (in "upper-limit" terms) today than there were forty years ago, and as noted above, recent rates of increase of scientific practitioners have perhaps reached a hundred a year. That such numbers have not only been placed in academic life, but that a considerable fraction of them have become regular contributors of research papers, is sufficient testimony to the self-sustaining quality of these fields in the recent past. However, this rapid growth has not been felt in the history of thought; indeed here there may have been not only a relative but an absolute decline in the number of practitioners. This subfield may very well have been running out of interesting puzzles. Perhaps the new questions of interpretation posed by the continuing growth of economics and of the history of science will serve to give it a new lease on life.[6]

If this brief sketch of economics as a social system is acceptable, then clearly the discipline passes Kuhn's tests. All this really means is that there are some striking similarities between the ways in which economists behave in their professional life and the behavior of natural scientists. The next step is to go a little further into the substance of the subject, in order to see if there are any peculiarities in its nature and practice which may distinguish it from so hard a natural science as, say, physics.

2

The Practice of Economics

In the last chapter it was argued that if one judges it by the standards which Kuhn has used in categorizing natural sciences, then economics passes muster as a science with flying colors. But some questions remain. Why is it that economists sometimes agree and sometimes disagree? Why are some sciences (and some parts of economics) hard, and others soft? How does one, scientifically speaking, come to know, and what sorts of things *can* one come to know? These are questions which will recur frequently in what follows. In the present chapter what is sought is a brief description of the processes of change in normal economics and of the factors that influence that change. The framework of the discussion remains that of Kuhn, especially his ingenious notion of a puzzle, though some shifts of emphasis and reinterpretation have been made to accommodate the special situation of a social science.[1] The five types of factors whose influence on the development of economics will be considered are puzzles, stylized facts, issues, the framework, and power.[2]

Puzzles

From the point of view of an active researcher, the heart of a science is a set of puzzles. These are problems which his fellow scientists believe to be both interesting and capable of solution. Like any set of puzzles, some are harder than others, and the status-rewards the correct solution entails for the puzzle-solving scientist are correspondingly higher for these. Kuhn has gone so far as to suggest that the desire to be identified by one's peers as an expert puzzle-solver is a primary motivation of most scientists.

There is certainly no dearth of puzzles in economics. Neoclassical economics can perhaps most easily be distinguished from the preceding classical school by means of just such a puzzle. Classical economists like Smith and Ricardo believed that the value of a commodity was measured by the amount of labor-time required to produce it. This idea seemed to work fairly well for some goods, but could not explain, for example, the very high prices and the wide fluctuations in price of well-known paintings. To classical economists such prices were simply anomalies to be explained as special cases. Neoclassical economists, such as Jevons and Marshall, were able to explain such prices easily within the general framework of supply and demand analysis. The solution to the puzzle came with the idea that prices are determined not by some averaging process but at the margin, thereby permitting an integrated treatment of the effects on prices of variations in both supply and demand. This particular puzzle-solution had an especially far-reaching effect on economics. Ever since, one of the really central processes in economic education has been development in the student of the ability to cast problems into this marginalist, supply-and-demand framework, so that the solution to the old puzzle has become a model for formulating new problems within the discipline.

A puzzle or two of current interest provides some further insight into the role of puzzles in economics. A macroeconomic puzzle emerged during the 1950's when the proliferating studies of consumption behavior began to show a systematic discrepancy. It was noticed that studies based on observations taken over a long period of time tended to differ systematically from those based on cross-section analysis of data from a given single time-period. The implication from the time-series data was that consumption tended to increase proportionately with income, while the cross-section data implied a less-than-proportionate increase of consumption with income. This was an interesting puzzle because economists at the time thought that they were observing essentially the same thing by these two procedures and expected to get similar results. Several theories were put forward as solutions to the problem, among the most interesting being that people tend to divide their income, both current and expected, into two parts, that which they will continue to receive more or less permanently and that which is essentially a windfall. The discrepancy between time-series and cross-section analysis was then explained by the relatively greater influence of windfall incomes on behavior in the latter case. Other factors also play a role in this situation, but general notions as to how to explain it are by now sufficiently integrated in the belief of economists that students can today be asked on standardized examinations to explain the discrepancy.[3]

Perhaps an even more revealing example of the way in which puzzles operate in economics comes from microeconomics. A standard proposition from the theory of the firm has it that shortrun business behavior will not be affected by a change in a proportionate tax on business income, such as the corporate income tax. The reasoning is that businessmen maximize profits; such a change does not alter the level of production and sales at which profits are maximized, but only changes the level of the maximum profits, which are still achieved at the same output level. One implication of this theory is that a corporate income tax levied as a proportion of profits could not be shifted by the corporation onto other participants in the market. This view has been challenged on the grounds that empirical evidence shows that shifting does in fact occur. The argument has been raging more or less continuously for a decade and has not yet subsided. Actually two different but related puzzles were posed in this controversy. One has to do with the question as to just what is meant by profit-maximizing behavior in the modern corporate setting and the relation of this behavior to tax shifting. The second puzzle is how to devise a statistical test for which data can be found and which will clearly distinguish varying degrees of shifting.[4]

Of these two examples, it is the tax puzzle that seems to be more typical of the situation in economics. Most economic problems deal with concepts whose fuzziness is a major handicap to a solution.[5] In the tax case, the problem is that economists don't really know how to distinguish profit maximization from other modes of behavior over a wide range of situations. Furthermore, the data that would be relevant are quite hard to come by. To understand a business decision, what one needs ideally is the set of facts and beliefs the businessman possessed at the time he made it. This can never be obtained, so a variety of indirect indices of what the practitioner thinks are likely to govern business decisions is substituted. Practitioners tend to differ persistently on the question as to which set of data is best for the problem. For reasons of this kind, which abound in economics, clearcut puzzles, and particularly clearcut consensual solutions to puzzles, are very hard to come by. Instead the ingenuity of the formulations and rationalizations of procedures tend to become the basis for judging the quality of scientific effort.

But this brings us back to that hierarchy of the first chapter, and to the core of theory which occupies its peak. Because this is where the status lies in economics, the practices developed there define the quality of procedures in applications. But to the extent that puzzles are not really solved, the system tends to become somewhat circular. The important thing becomes not so much to solve the puzzle as to make an ingenious attempt at solving it within the conventional framework of puzzles. There is thus some risk that economic science may degenerate into a series of self-contained methodological explorations which are not closely tied to that real world which is the nominal subject of investigation.

The central role that such puzzles play in the normal development of economics is clear. They serve to focus the attention of a number of researchers on a particular problem area, since there is usually widespread agreement that a particular puzzle is in fact a puzzle, and other members of the profession will be excited and impressed by a solution, or even by one of those ingenious attempts. This tends to provide a bunching of research effort in those areas in which the science has a felt need for further enlightenment. Described in this way, it sounds like economics and other sciences are examples of near-optimal social systems, with an amazing ability to concentrate resources where they are most needed, to get very broad agreement as to what scientific need is, and to provide individual incentives that encourage scientists to try to do just what the science needs to have done.

Stylized Facts

Another factor that exerts considerable influence on the way economics develops is a somewhat peculiar one, not much discussed in methodological treatises. It is the existence of stylized facts that focus attention in precisely the *opposite* sense as puzzles: that is, these are false or at least exaggerated assumptions about some of the facts of the situation under study which are designed to get the researcher's attention *away* from these facts and onto others. In good studies, these stylized-fact assumptions are restricted to ones that are in effect licensed by the profession, so that economists reading the particular study will have already been prepared by their past training and experience to live with the assumptions.

An example or two will illustrate the way this phenomenon works in economics. One of the most hallowed stylized facts of econometric investigations is that "strange observations don't count." A time-series study will not be dismissed because it does not try to explain what happened during World War II, even though it does try to explain what happened before and after that event. The reasoning is clear enough: the structure of the economy was so different during the war that explanatory factors will be different or at least have different weights. Consequently, trying to put these observations into the study may only serve to bias the estimation of causal factors operating during more normal times. Now everyone knows that all years are "strange" to some extent and that a really good model would welcome the stronger tests that extreme observations can offer; but the qualified students go along with this game because it is their judgment that, on balance, some strange observations do more harm than good. And of course they expect both to have to defend any particular application of the strangeness rule, and to be treated symmetrically by the profession in their own applications of the rule.[6]

Studies are not obliged to make use of any particular widely used stylized fact. It is a matter of convenience, of where the researcher wants to focus his attention, and to what extent he thinks he might get in trouble if he does make that particular false assumption. A researcher concentrating on the effect of controls on aggregative economic activity is less likely to exclude World War II than a student of the private investment sector. Some stylized facts, however, are not quite so obvious in their impact as the strangeness rule. For example, it is customary in studying many aspects of consumer behavior to assume that preferences are stable in the sense that tastes for goods and services don't change. Economists are well aware that this *is* a stylized fact, that it is often wrong. And there are some studies in which changes in preferences are admitted. But studies that find it convenient to make this assumption are not very likely to be criticized from within the science for this particular stylized fact, because of its familiarity to economists from their training and because of its centrality to the basic normative propositions of welfare economics. Any serious and systematic critique of this stylized fact would be striking at the heart of neoclassical economics. This raises the question: To what extent are stylized facts used to conceal anomalies, to discourage consideration of topics in ways that would be destructive of the framework of consensus of economic science?

Issues

Though atom bombs and the like have changed the situation somewhat, social sciences have generally been thought to differ substantially from natural sciences in the directness with which current events influence their development. Clearly, many of the properties of a scientific social system have the effect of isolating the invisible college of scientists from the outside world. How does this work out in economics? To what extent does the invisible college work as a barrier to influences from the current scene?

The most natural way for economics to be affected from outside is by the issues of the day that are relevant for economic science. That there is such an influence cannot be doubted. A glance at the index of economic journals shows clearly that when there is war there are more articles in economic journals dealing with war. When in the early postwar period the stabilization of the international monetary system was of considerable public concern, there were more articles on this topic. During the depression the number of articles dealing with depression-related matters increased.

But issues have a different form depending on the public before which they are being aired. For example, toward the end of the nineteenth century the question whether the United States should remain on a bimetallic standard or go over to the gold standard became a major national issue, dominating at least one Presidential election and eliciting some of our political history's purplest prose. Basically the issue tended to pit debtors (farmers and the poor) against creditors (the rich), the former fearing that the gold standard implied a hard-money, even deflationary policy, and the latter probably hoping that that was the case. However, some wealthier interests, like silver mine owners, favored bimetallism for fairly obvious reasons, and out west, where the silver mine owners were located and powerful, it could cost an economist his job to oppose the policy.

This issue did exercise economists, but they tended to talk about it in a very different way than did the general public. The neoclassical economist's orientation was transformed by his discipline into emphasis on the quantity theory of money and its international application. In this framework the key question was how to avoid tipover effects from changes in the relative international price of the two moneys under bimetallism. Though many economists were sincerely concerned about the equity issue, it was the technical issue which was much the more interesting from the point of view of economic science, and it tended to dominate neoclassical economists' discussions. In a word, the tipover problem was a scientific puzzle, the equity question was not. Thus issues of public policy can and often do influence the course of economic discussion, but the transformation they undergo from the one public to the other, conditioned as it is in our case by the very nature of the invisible college of economists, can be quite substantial.

The Framework

There is more to the "network of commitments," as Kuhn calls them, of the invisible college of economists than their attitudes toward puzzles, stylized facts, and issues. Economics is a liberal profession, and almost all of the college's members at major institutions in the United States are liberals, both by self-avowal and by philosophical orientation. The connection between anything as broad as liberal philosophy and anything as precise as economic science is not so easy to establish, but let us at least try to characterize succinctly the main elements of traditional liberal belief and see to what extent these beliefs are to be found in the intellectual traditions of economics.[7]

Traditional liberal psychology is based on three principles: hedonism, rationalism, and atomism. Hedonism or the Benthamite pleasure-pain principle characterizes man in terms of drive-reduction or the satisfaction of the urgent demands of the body and mind; there is a clear corollary of natural indolence that follows fairly directly from the avoidance of pain. Rationalism is means-ends orientation, the use of deliberative choice among alternatives in seeking the satisfactions of drive-reduction. Atomism is the assertion of the essential separateness and autonomy of each man from every other, with the consequent stabilization of values by means of processes internal to the individual human organism.

The political theory of liberalism is emotionally in tune with its psychology. The state is viewed as a device to provide certain kinds of services that are necessary and would not otherwise be forthcoming, that has no other justification than this, and that is likely to be a threat to the realization of other needs of the citizenry. Among the functions of the state are to provide protection against the vices and violence of others and to foster a framework in which productivity is encouraged. Various safeguards are to be built into the state to prevent excessive use of the coercive power, the strongest of these being the judicial protection of the individual's civil rights and the admission of the right of revolution of the citizens against a state which is patently failing to provide the services for which it was, in principle, instituted.

In the economy the liberal espouses the doctrine of harmony of interests among elements of the citizenry. This harmony is to be exercised through the freedoms of the market place, and the protection by the state of resources privately accumulated as a result of the exercise of those freedoms. In certain cases the state may substitute for the market where the society's welfare is patently fostered thereby.

The close relation between liberal and neoclassical economic styles of argument, as reflected in the puzzles and stylized facts of economic science, seems clear enough. The model of liberal man is exemplified in the theory of consumption which appears in all the economic textbooks and informs a great deal of the research. The liberal model of the state fits perfectly the conceptions of public finance, in which the state is conceived as a set of taxing and/or spending agencies, often treated as mutually independent, each of which is making certain cost-benefit calculations with respect to the services it provides. The autonomous individuals of economics come into conflict, but this conflict is dramatically transformed by the bargaining processes of the market place into a harmony of interests, a Pareto-optimality in principle, whose liberal credentials are impeccable. Clearly there is a very close connection between the harmony-of-interests thesis and contemporary welfare-economics, with the latter's emphasis on the normative properties of an abstract model of competitive capitalism in which the impersonal operation of the market resolves *all* conflicts of professional interest to economists. Even the political theory that has crept into economics in recent years is one in which the achievement of a state in which all participants have already accepted the rules of the game and are thereby constrained to the bargaining-compromise resolution of their differences simply goes without saying. The analysis begins from there. One might also note an optimistic overtone to the whole operation which, though it is not necessarily a liberal feature (some liberals are rather pessimistic) nevertheless is equally an overtone of liberal philosophy. In both cases the general feeling that pervades both the science and the philosophy is that things can be worked out.

These connections can easily be traced out in the history of the science, which in fact was historically an offshoot of the general liberal philosophical tradition. Nevertheless, a rather widespread view has grown up among economists that basic economic theory is value-neutral, that it can be applied to any society, and that in principle it can be made to serve almost any political ends. This notion will be appraised at several points in what follows. At the moment it is perhaps relevant to point out that it is by no means the case that there is no reasonable alternative to the liberal position. In fact, there is a collection of views which at almost every turn opposes the liberal preconceptions and which has been around in social thought since the turn of the century and before. In brief, these views emphasize the role of consciousness in the interpretation of personality, the role of interaction in the interpretation of politics, and the role of conflict in the interpretation of both the economy and the polity. Its orientation is often, though not always, pessimistic and is at least prepared to admit as a question worthy of analysis the hypothesis that progress breeds not welfare but catastrophe.

In their modern form these views were developed by what Stuart Hughes has called the generation of the 90's, including such men as Freud, Durkheim, Pareto, Jung, Croce, and others.[8] In the next few sentences we extract a hybrid "essence" of this collection of views, sufficiently accurate, we hope, to make the point that there *are* alternatives to liberalism that are not *prima facie* absurd or morally reprehensible. The notion of man is that of an organism struggling toward wholeness against the fragmentation his environment increasingly inflicts on him, an organism whose self-awareness is not always reliable, an organism whose differences from liberal man are suggested in the slogan: Not Rationalism but Rationalizing. The political theory emphasizes the forces that promote solidarity, that do not require the mediation of bargaining because, for good or ill, they represent internalized values of the members of society. But at the same time there is a recognition of the fundamental role that conflict plays in social processes, of the fact that common value-systems typically inhere in segments of a polity rather than in the whole, and that consequently the study of social-value generation, of conflict processes, and of the interdependent relation of economy and polity is essential to a scientific framework suitable to this world-view of society. But this is a picture of the world and of the role of man in it that contradicts at obvious places the orientation of neoclassical economics. Consequently it appears that the framework of economic science is far from being psychologically, philosophically, politically, or economically neutral.

Power

Once one accepts the notion that a science is a social system, it is hard to avoid the prospect that there are instruments available to make it worth a scientist's while to do one thing and costly to do another. In the case of economics it is easy enough to see what the instruments are, though not quite so easy to get a feel for the extent to which they are applied in practice. In this section we are concerned merely to list the major nonsubstantive ways in which economists may be influenced in their choice of activities.

First, and most obvious of all, an economist may choose his activities because of a primary desire to improve economic science. As a normal scientist he would presumably apply the principle of comparative advantage in matching his own skills and interests to the currently outstanding puzzles in the discipline.

A second motivation may be simple ambition. An economist who wishes to get ahead is encouraged by the reward system to simulate as closely as possible the choices of a selfless scientist. This does not produce the same result, however. The careerist is likely to get into administration early in his career; he may try to team up with a "selfless" or at least more competent type in order to raise the average quality of the work attributed to him. And perhaps most important, he is relatively more strongly oriented toward the ingenuity of his solutions and less toward genuine advancement of the science.

Despite these careerist possibilities, there is a surprisingly good match between intrinsically and extrinsically motivated behaviors in economics, and apparently in most normal science, as compared with many other social systems. The reason for this is that the censors who eliminate from professional consideration some work and who allocate praise among the acceptable studies, are themselves extremely competent. Indeed, they tend to be among the leaders of the profession, men whose status has been acquired by the high quality of the work they have performed as judged by the profession's current and quondam leaders. As recognized leaders, their judgments on the acceptability of proposed puzzles and solutions are often decisive.

The power inherent in this system of quality control within the economics profession is obviously very great. The discipline's censors occupy leading posts in economics departments at the major institutions, and their students and lesser confrères occupy similar posts at nearly all the universities that train new Ph.D.'s. The lion's share of appointment [9] and dismissal power has been vested in the departments themselves at these institutions. Any economist with serious hopes of obtaining a tenured position in one of these departments will soon be made aware of the criteria by which he is to be judged. In a word, he is expected to become a normal economic scientist.[10]

Of course it is not true, as the last paragraph may seem to imply, that this decision as to whether to become a normal science economist is made at the stage in his career at which the economist has obtained his last degree. For, as in all normal sciences, the entire academic program, beginning usually at the undergraduate level but certainly at the graduate, consists of indoctrination in the ideas and techniques of the science. As much as anything, this is a self-selection process. Those who do not accept the basic ideas of the science will not proceed very far with its study. Standards for admission to economic science are not terribly demanding, comparatively speaking; consequently those who drop out of the system, at least in the author's experience, are not typically intellectual failures. Rather they are those who have become "turned off," and their most common complaint is lack of relevance, not difficulty.

These inside instruments of control are accompanied by outside instruments exercised by members of the larger society. Probably the most important of these is control of funds for research and, to a lesser extent, teaching. Foundations and government agencies have their own (often overlapping) priorities, and the more expensive kinds of economic research are often only possible with their help.

Though economists typically participate in allocation decisions, basic priorities are usually laid down at a higher level than that at which the economist-consultant operates.

Finally, there is politically motivated direct intervention in the processes of normal science. In principle this can take the form of jailing economists, dismissing them regardless of the judgment of their scientific peers, suppression of publication, and the like. All these things of course happen to neoclassical economists, though it is quite a rare phenomenon in the United States. More subtly, such outside pressures stem from the political activities and commitments of the profession's leaders, many of whom have close ties to Washington. This is inevitably restrictive of behavior and interests and may easily find some reflection in the ways in which these leaders use the great power they possess to shape careers and determine research priorities within the discipline.[11]

Conclusion

The discussion of this chapter suggests that economic science develops along a sharply constrained trajectory. The motive-force for development is the emergence of puzzles, which in turn is caused by the proposing of solutions to previous puzzles, and by transforming the issues of the time into the language of economic science. Constraints to the path of development come from the focusing devices, including the evolving tradition of acceptable stylized facts, the underlying world-view economists have in common, and the constraints imposed by power in the normal science social system and its environment.

If our picture is reasonably accurate there is no question but that economics *is* a science in the Kuhnian sense. Nevertheless, there are important aspects of its procedure that are rather troubling. The fact that a science should be so closely tied to an ideology is perhaps the most important of these troubling aspects. Any fears aroused by this are bound to be enhanced by recognition of the possibility that though economics generates new puzzles, it often, perhaps typically, does not solve the old ones, and that methodological sophistication may often substitute for solution in the eyes of the most respected practitioners. And still more fears will come from recognition of the possibilities afforded by stylized facts and the power of insiders to control the trajectory of the science by focusing practitioners' attention on areas that are consistent with the survival of the existing structure, social and substantive, of the science.

3

A Science in Crisis?

Every now and then the processes of normal science break down, and some rather dramatic changes occur in the way in which practitioners view some important aspects of their subject. Kuhn calls the periods in which changes of this sort occur, "scientific revolutions," and attributes a number of general properties to them, of which the following are perhaps the most important:

1 A novel theory emerges within normal science only after a pronounced failure in the normal science's problem-solving activity.
2 An important sign of the breakdown of normal science is the proliferation of theories and of methodological discussion.
3 The problems with respect to which breakdown occurs are all of a type that had long been recognized by practitioners.
4 The actual solution to a crisis has been at least partially anticipated earlier, but in the absence of crisis those anticipations had been ignored.
5 The general intellectual framework of a normal science, including the puzzles, stylized facts, and research techniques, as well as the fuzzier commitments associated with its

world-view, has a powerful inertial effect on the scientist who has absorbed it. This is of course highly functional for normal science but greatly complicates revolutions. Older scientists usually do not absorb revolutions.

6 A new and competing scientific framework redefines a number of puzzles and may also generate new puzzles. A puzzle in the old framework may become a counterexample in the new. An anomaly in the old theory may simply be a fact in the new one. Hence adherents to old and new tend to talk past one another.

7 The new theory emerges over a limited period of time. The full emergence of a crisis and of a solution which begins to attract adherents may take a decade or two. It takes another and longer period of time to work out the implications of the new framework.

8 Scientists who succeed in making the transition from old to new often report their experience as being rather like a mystic conversion, though it need not come in a flash as with many religious conversions.

The Keynesian Revolution

Several economists have recently noticed the similarity between certain changes in economics, particularly the advent and development of Keynesian economics, and the Kuhnian picture of a scientific revolution.[1] We may review very briefly some of the major changes that occurred before and after the appearance of the General Theory in 1936 as an introduction to the processes by which "abnormal" change can occur in economic science.[2]

The principal anomalies that were emerging in the 20's and early 30's that were relevant for Keynesian economics came in monetary theory and capital theory. For the former, the basic problem was that though neoclassical economics stood, more than anything else, for analysis in terms of supply and demand, money remained outside this analysis. Many rather confused statements about money can be found in the 20's, a common thread being that money is not really a commodity, since its only function is to produce barter on a more efficient basis. Nevertheless, it was clear that there was some sort of relationship between shortrun fluctuations in economic behavior, and the amount of money available to the economy and its use by the citizens. This anomaly was moving slowly to the foreground, and theories were proliferating, but no integration of real and monetary phenomena had yet occurred within the science which would accept important causal interactions between the two spheres.

Capital theory faced a similar problem—how to take account of the monetary factors that influenced investment decisions—the standard theory putting exclusive emphasis on real factors such as productivity of capital and the time-pattern of preferences. There had been a great proliferation of theories in the two or three decades preceding the General Theory, but no resolution.

A rather different kind of anomaly was posed by the status of business-cycle analysis within conventional economics. As a leading historian of the economic thought of the period has noted, the study of business cycles tended to be a peripheral subject, the specialization of economists who were not particularly sympathetic to the neoclassical orientation, or at least did not apply it much in their work.[3] The reason for this peculiar status was that the business cycle was not "interesting" in neoclassical terms, since the subject it studied was anomalous. It studied variations in the level of economic activity that were certain, according to neoclassical theory, to be corrected by the operation of market forces. Also, the practitioners by and large did not try to develop theories which could seriously challenge the existing structure of belief.

It is probably hard for someone not trained in neoclassical economics to understand how economists could let their theory get them into the situation of believing that the variation in the level of output was not an interesting phenomenon for study and analysis. There is no need here to describe that situation, for it is a fact accepted by students of the period and well described elsewhere.[4] Indeed, the situation is even more surprising, for there were in fact a number of theories that did analyze variation in the level of output, some of them in a very Keynesian way, but these theories were "underworld" phenomena, in Keynes's apt phrase, the products of writers who were not acceptable as members of the invisible college.[5] Their works were ignored or dismissed with contempt.

Economics is influenced by more than its set of puzzles, however, and the Keynesian revolution clearly exemplifies the role that current issues can play in such a science. For the great factual anomaly of the period was the persistence of massive unemployment, which in England had already developed in the 20's. This fact did not contradict the neoclassical theory: it would be explained there in terms of frictions and resistances to wage and price changes, particularly by labor. A neoclassical economist could satisfy himself theoretically with a slogan such as, "The longer the unemployment, the stronger the monopoly unions." This view in fact persisted among many neoclassical economists, especially among those who were middle-aged by the 30's.

Nevertheless a problem remained: what to *do* about the

unemployment. Not only was it politically infeasible to do nothing, it was positively dangerous. There were, after all, those unconventional theories about what to do, and the idea that informed many of them—that if you simply give people more money they will spend it, and that is a move toward prosperity—was a difficult one to refute in the language of laymen. And there were in the wings not only unconventional theories but unconventional political groupings with even more drastic remedies to propose. It was not just a case of misbehaving atoms that could be studied at one's leisure. What was needed politically was a theory that explained what was wrong, explained what to do about it, and whose policy prescriptions were politically feasible for the existing political parties.

Keynes was admirably equipped for both the political and the scientific job. He held the most prestigious chair of economics in the Anglo-American world and was a specialist in the subject in which the theoretical anomalies were most visible. He had previously grappled with these anomalies and by 1930 had already acquired somewhat unconventional, if not fully coherent, views on the subject. He was politically active, was well aware of the nature and operation of the British political system, and had an established reputation as a prescient iconoclast. Furthermore, he had been advocating the basic Keynesian policies for some years, and their political feasibility was not really in question in a land with as large a welfare system as Britain had. Indeed, in his more pessimistic moments, Keynes's lament was not that the politicians would not buy his approach, but that the central bankers would not. In the early 30's what was lacking of the three factors mentioned in the last paragraph was only the first: a theory that would explain what was already believable and feasible policy.

The "Keynesian revolution" did clearly bring the study of variations in the level of aggregate output into the center of conventional economics. In our asserted hierarchy of contemporary fields in Chapter 1, macroeconomics, which embraces this topic as its central problem, is now right up there with the leaders, whereas a decade or two before Keynes it was close to being a Class D field. Furthermore, Keynes played a very important role in developing a theory of money in terms of supply and demand, so that one major anomaly of the older theory has virtually disappeared. Quite aside from the political and policy impact, Keynesianism has dramatically changed some of the major ways in which economists view their subject.

Nevertheless, there are some persistent problems which are perhaps not so apparent on the surface of the subject—for example in the textbooks—but which suggest that Keynesianism was less than a revolution. For one thing, changing the status of macroeconomics from an underworld topic to a high-status one has by no means meant that it has become integrated with the main body of economic theory. Micro and macro remain two distinct theories, and the propositions of one are not derivable from the propositions of the other.[6] Second, there are quite a few "Keynesian" economists who believe that the upshot of the years of discussion of the theory is a general recognition that the chief culprit in persistent unemployment situations is rigidity in prices and wages; but this is not so very different from the older neoclassical position. There has clearly been a good deal of development of understanding of the ways in which price rigidity works, but as the principal causal factor, it remains in essentially its pre-Keynesian status. Third, despite the change in monetary theory, the old dichotomy between real and monetary phenomena remains; no clearer picture of this can be found than in the persistent difficulties in integrating the two successfully in the large scale, empirically estimated models that are widely regarded as the crowning accomplishment of shortrun macroeconomics. The textbook version of Keynesianism (the "IS-LM" diagram) suggests an interactive mechanism between real and monetary factors that is neither empirically verified nor even plausible to many conventional practitioners. Finally, one might note that though Keynes himself deplored the approach, the Keynesian theory has seemed to lend itself to Mechanical Marvel theorizing: to the formulation of models based on the complex interaction of a very small number of variables, each of which represents an aggregate whose real-world stability depends more on the law of large numbers than on any established economic principle. The paradigm Mechanical Marvel was Samuelson's famous multiplier-accelerator interaction, but the tendency for this sort of thing to proliferate wildly beyond the ability of anyone to vouch for its connection with the real world has been one of the major features of recent economics. Thus has Keynesianism, the policy-oriented discipline *par excellence,* been transformed into something very like its neoclassical predecessor of the 20's, a field in which rationalism tends to substitute for empiricism, theoretical sophistication for common sense.

In summary Keynes, because of his great influence in both political and economic circles, was able to convince major segments of both groups that a well-known and common-sense solution to the problem of unemployment was indeed the best one to apply. As an intellectual by-product of this, his greatest essay in persuasion, mainline economics was forced to rethink the whole area of aggregative economics, money, and capital theory, so as to incorporate changes in the level of output into the picture. This was a difficult process and took the better part of two decades. At its end much of what Keynes proposed in the General Theory had either been dropped or remained controversial, but aggregative economics and most of its key concepts, such as money and savings and investment, would never be the same again. Within economics the Keynesian revolution was definitely a Kuhnian revolution, though revolution is too strong a word to apply to the Keynesian impact on western economies and polities.[7]

Another Revolution?

The postwar period has seen a change in the mental set of mainline economists which I think must be ranked by the practitioners themselves as a revolution that is more profound than the Keynesian, though there are connections between the two. This one might be called the formalist revolution. The conventional interwar theorist was not at home with mathematics; he preferred verbal analysis, and there was in many practitioners a certain rationalistic bias which tended to keep empirical facts out of the central places in their arguments. The applied economist, on the other hand, was likely to have a strong historical bent and did not make a great deal of direct use of the products of the theorists. Today this rationalist-historical mix has virtually disappeared. The contemporary theorist is not only well-grounded in mathematics, but finds it the natural medium for expressing his professional ideas: the proof has replaced the argument.[8] The well-regarded applied economist still knows his field of application, but his orientation is no longer historical. Instead, he seeks ways of formulating hypotheses which have the twin properties of being related to interesting modern theory and of being capable of statistical test. His aim is not so much to build a picture of events and their causes from historical documents as it is to test hypotheses of theoretical interest by using statistical tools and a pool of discovered or generated "empirical" numbers. The reader probably does not need to be persuaded that the orientations of these two different sets of economists, the rationalist-historical and the formalist, are very different. In training and in their stock of factual information they are more different than typical practitioners of adjacent natural sciences. The frequency with which graduate students are recruited to economics from history and political science has declined substantially, and the incidence of students whose backgrounds are in mathematics and physics has correspondingly increased. The pattern of on-campus contacts and friendships across departments has changed in the same direction. Even the style of humor has changed.[9]

One might argue that this revolution in research style grew out of an anomaly that was becoming increasingly apparent during the interwar period. Certainly there were a number of criticisms of the failure to integrate theory and practice, and an historian's lament that, as far as his work was concerned, economic theory had done no more than construct a set of empty boxes, gave a new concept to economics.[10] The pressure for change may have been increased by the quite rapid spread of the positivist view of science during this period, and the lamentable defects that economics displayed by this standard. Clearly some sort of groping toward the formalist solution was in progress. However, though there had been a number of mathematically oriented economists in the past, they were isolated and their work was for the most part somewhat crotchety. Perhaps the first thoroughly modern economic theorist was Frank Ramsey, who published several profound papers before his early death in 1931. Statistics too had its proponents and practitioners, though the connections with economics remained somewhat distant. But again, key works were published in the 30's that were distinctly modern in their approach, perhaps none more so than Tinbergen's great 1939 monograph on business cycles.

If one accepts such signs as sufficient support for the existence of a Kuhnian crisis, it is a relatively easy step to the assertion that this crisis was resolved in the first postwar decade. Today, the integration between theory and application has become complete, at least in principle, and theorists and applied mainline economists in the central fields not only can but do communicate easily with one another. The new ways have spread until they dominate all the major American and English training schools for research Ph.D.'s. The whole field of economics, or at least all parts of it that can be fitted to the mold, have been or are in the process of being rethought in terms of the new procedures; in the process many terms have acquired new shadings of meaning as they are tied to newly formalized systems of theory. Many puzzles which had popped up before as a result of the quantitative imprecision of the mother tongue have either dropped from sight or been turned into homework problems for students.[11] And it all happened rather suddenly. Starting as a new social system of formalists working together at Chicago and M.I.T. in the late 40's, it spread to other schools within a decade or so, and by the early 60's, all economics departments with any interest in research were feverishly stocking up on the new breed economists. By about 1965 something approaching a new steady state had been reached, and a new normal-science economics was moving forward serenely under its new banners.

This sounds like about as classic a case of a Kuhnian scientific revolution as one could imagine. And yet there is one striking and anomalous feature to the whole transformation of economics: it was essentially methodological rather than substantive. If one accepts the Keynesian revolution as a phenomenon of the 30's and 40's, and the formalist revolution as a phenomenon of the 50's and 60's, there just are not any fundamental substantive changes of direction brought about by the latter. The core of theory remains the analysis of the price system, and right at its heart is still to be found the competitive régime of production and exchange. Associated with this theory is Keynesian economics and growth theory, whose basic ideas were well-known by 1950.[12] In applied work much the same is true, though the very great increase in the amount of data available describing the economy has, in combination with the manifold increase in the number of practitioners, given contemporary economists a much more detailed picture of certain aspects of the economy than was available to our predecessors. But again, dramatically new ideas are just not there. It is as if the interwar economists had some sort of uncanny ability to intuit the features that are now being traced out in more detail. The great methodological puzzle in economics is why a great methodological revolution should make so little substantive difference.

Generations and Events

If there *is* a major substantive difference between old and new economics it is in the substantially greater normative emphasis of the new. Part of this is clearly attributable to a change in the environment within which economics functions—for example, a large government means many more problems in public-finance policy. The Keynesian revolution did its part as well, and became even more relevant as the increasing size of government magnified its potential impact on the level of economic activity. But the change is much more dramatic than this. Economists have become a necessary part of the staff of the larger corporations and trade unions. In government they not only advise on matters of tax policy and the multiplier, but have become specialists in educational and medical and even defense "economics." As these interests have grown up, the discipline has responded with its array of mathematical and statistical tools, providing a normal scientific basis for the policy effort. And as the data have become more massive and complex, policymakers turn with increasing frequency to economists to help them understand the problems they face.

Certain aspects of this change may well be the result

of orientations acquired by practitioners simply because of their generational affiliation, and particularly because of the impact of a few key events on their lives and work. Naturally assertions of this kind are rather speculative, but most of them have been made at least in casual conversation by other economists, and some individual stories known to me lend support to others.

First, consider the homelands of interwar and postwar economics. The former was clearly England, where Pigou and Keynes led colleagues and students firmly along the Marshallian path, with Hicks in essentially the same tradition, and the London School of Economics and the redbricks displaying all the traits of followers. The Keynesian revolution was a revolution from above. It quickly caught the fancy of the younger economists and spread from there across the ocean to America. In the United States there was a more eclectic atmosphere, but this was shattered during the postwar period, when economists in the United States assumed the lead in the formalist revolution and American academic departments of economics became, relative to their past, rigid adherents to the new orthodoxy. The formalist revolution was also a revolution from above, led by men whose academic position marked them already as leaders. But by and large they were not American economists: a surprising fraction of the leaders, clearly more than half, were educated on the Continent. What they brought with them to the United States was a tradition hardly known in either of the Anglo-American bastions of neoclassical economics, one which culminated in the 40's and 50's in the new general equilibrium analysis, game theory, the theory of planning, econometrics, and an already developed formalist tradition. America became the land of heterotic vigor, with students and faculty alike exposed to both the Marshallián and Walrasian traditions, the English and the Continental, and thus forced by circumstances to seek some amalgam.

The generation of economists in which these teachings were most keenly felt was inevitably a transition generation. Only a modest fraction of its members both received the necessary exposure and possessed the necessary intellectual qualities to seize the opportunity. But another factor was operating on them, one which may have been even more important in shaping postwar economics. For these students were the product of two extraordinary formative experiences: the Great Depression and World War II. The first of these shook rather definitively any remaining faith in the autonomous, self-adjusting features of the capitalist system. For them it became instead an article of faith that things could easily go very badly wrong. The war, on the other hand, preached a rather optimistic message. A Great Evil had come into the world, and organized effort had brought about its destruction. Furthermore, the instrument for this great triumph of Good over Evil was none other than that peculiarly inefficient government bureaucracy, the United States Armed Forces. As participants in the war, this generation of economists could top anyone's story of bureaucratic folly; but even so, that fumbling bureaucracy worked. The emotional, psychological message from these two great events was a clear one: the world must be managed if it is to work at all, and even the incredibly cumbersome and inefficient bureaucracies that were all that was available could be made to do the job.

Whichever of the two factors may have been the more important—failure to imbibe the new intellectual spirit while still at a malleable age, or the influence of the two key events—a relatively large fraction of this generation did not become fully converted to formalist economics, and the gap in their corpus of work is plainly visible in most economics departments. Instead, they tended to become more action-oriented or policy-oriented, to serve as go-betweens for economic scientists and policymakers, to spend much time as consultants to government and foundations, and even to become deeply involved in university administration.[13]

No doubt this gave a considerable fillip to the already-prominent policy-orientation of the postwar discipline. Nothing makes one more interested in policy than the thought that one might be able to influence it. But it also had another consequence, which may well have been of substantial impact within the discipline. As a result of their somewhat nonmainline orientation, the work of modernization, of resolution of the formalist crisis, tended to an extraordinary extent to skip a generation. The great men of the older generation passed their wisdom along to a modest fraction of the next or policy-oriented generation, but widespread involvement in the new science was reserved for the generation presently in their thirties and a little beyond. My guess, and it is no more than that, as to the impact of this peculiar age distribution of effort, is that it has been narrowing and technicizing. The intellectual function of the intermediate generation, which would have led the research of the 60's from a firm base of previous accomplishment and a consequent broad awareness of pitfalls and blind alleys, would have been to pass along this hard-won knowledge to the younger generation in a form that was usable by a modern technician, and to control the excesses of formalism. Without such guidance, the predictable errors have indeed occurred.

Permanent Revolution

Kuhn's description of normal science seems to imply clearly that all normal science is "marginalist": change proceeds step by step without provoking dramatic changes in the central orientations of scientists. This is good news for the science that coined the term "marginalism," and whose intellectual orientation is so fundamentally linked with the appraisal of alternatives that do not differ substantially from one another. And there was more good news in the history of economics since about the mid-50's, a period in which the processes of normal development within the formalist framework were indeed producing a tremendous proliferation of studies of normal science problems of detail. Never in its previous history had economics shown such unanimity among its practitioners as to the nature and prospects of the discipline.

Nevertheless, the history of this same period can be recounted as a period of developing crisis. There were indeed a number of scandals, as Arrow has called them,[14] of recognized puzzles or anomalies that research has not succeeded in dealing with effectively. The failure to provide any sort of integration of microeconomics and macroeconomics has already been mentioned. Another scandal has been the failure to produce any sort of satisfying analysis of imperfect competition within a general equilibrium framework, any scientifically acceptable analyses of the interaction of relatively largescale economic organizations with the rest of their environment. Third on Arrow's list, and most important on mine, was the failure to take reasonable account of the cost of making transactions in theories; the tremendous impact that information, knowledge, and understanding have on the economic process is essentially ignored.

To this list, a number of other failings may be added. We seem to be able to perceive now an upper limit to the productivity of additional data in improving the quality of econometric studies, and the limit is emerging at a level of accomplishment which is not strikingly superior to that achieved by the well-informed intuitive observer. Mathematics can be a curse as well as a blessing, defining puzzle quality in terms of mathematical rather than economic standards and thereby raising serious questions of scientific relevance with respect to much of this work. Again, mathematical economics can be theorem-seeking rather than truth-seeking. Externalities are a scandal in themselves; since the early 50's there has been no substantial progress in developing a satisfying technique for dealing with problems whose significance is beginning to dwarf the problems which can be fitted into the "classical" framework of assumptions. The obviously strong interactions of most economic variables with noneconomic factors receives, at best, fitful attention. And finally, there is the question of distribution, on which modern, normal economic science continues to remain uneasily silent, fearing to transcend on the one hand the positivist norm of avoiding value-judgments, and unable on the other to think of anything interesting of a "positive" nature to say.

As one runs through the list of anomalies in contemporary economic science, the thought occurs inescapably that these are not emerging problems: most of them have been around for decades, though the relative importance of each has been variable. Despite all those signs of Kuhnian normality, can it be that economics is in a state of permanent revolution, in which the tensions of unsolved problems continually percolate on the fringes of a discipline that studiously ignores them while continuing the development of its problems of detail? [15]

Laws as Variables

Immanuel Velikovsky is a name well known to science fiction fans, though his work was not intended as science fiction. Velikovsky, trained as a philologist, became convinced that ancient stories of the Flood and of other catastrophes, some of them accompanied by dramatic changes in the configuration of the heavens, were not myth but genuine history.[16] For this to be true the laws of physics and astronomy would have to have been different in ancient times than they are today; that is, the actual behavior of the earth and the stars would have to have been governed by different laws in those days.

So far as I know, no reputable physicist has endorsed Velikovsky's views, but suppose for the moment that he is right. What would be the implications for physics? Clearly the study of the subject would have to begin to take account of the possibility that a change in its basic laws could occur at any time, and in particular, new variables would have to be sought out which might hold the key to such changes. Relatively less effort would be devoted to studying those problems of detail if it were expected that such work had relevance over only a limited time-period.

Every physicist engaged in such work would be beset by the nagging fear that he was working on a topic that was about to become of merely antiquarian interest. More effort would be devoted to the fuzzier but now important task of seeking out a new set of underlying factors which might help return the study of physical phenomena to a more normal course, at least for a while.

This is a matter of at best casual interest to a physicist. But for economists things are different, for we are all well aware that economists *do* live in a Velikovskyan world, that our laws are subject to frequent and even sudden change, that nature is constantly taking back some portion of the information we have won from her over the years about the economy. For example, few econometricians believe that the quality of our understanding of contemporary short-term functioning of the American economy would be aided much by using interwar observations, and many believe that they are likely to do more harm than good. The structure of the economy has changed drastically since then and some interactions which were valid then are different now, so that the old data may be positively misleading. All of the aggregative concepts such as consumption and investment tend to lose their significance as longer time-periods are brought under consideration because the nature and mix of the goods included in these concepts changes so rapidly from one decade to the next. The microeconomic world, too, has changed dramatically; the quality and amount of information available to consumers and businessmen today compared to thirty or forty years ago will serve as an example of structural change in this area—a change which has considerable effect on the usefulness of models of decision-making behavior.

This is not, I am sure, a controversial assertion. Everyone knows that it is going on and that it is important. The interesting question is rather, Why does economics continue to act as if it were studying phenomena with the properties of real-time physics when it is in fact dealing with a Velikovskyan world?

An answer to this question has been foreshadowed in earlier sections of this work. Most important is the connection between the liberal philosophical commitment and the structure of economics. Economics can preserve such a close connection and survive as a science because of the peculiar difficulties in bringing off conclusive solutions to its puzzles. The emphasis on methodological definition of puzzles is the giveaway to both the Velikovskyan nature of the subject and to its ability to simulate normal scientific procedures despite this property. Liberal principles can guide the normal science regardless of the facts, because the facts are so hard to come by that crucial ones are rarely confuted by studies.

The marginalist orientation is also closely related to another property of the discipline: its intimate association with the preservation of the basic structure of society. The United States, indeed the western developed world, is operated under the aegis of liberal, middle-class orientations. Economic science, with its extraordinarily high component of normative studies, is primarily concerned with assisting the process of control and adjustment of that society. Economics is one of the most highly developed of policy sciences, but the insistence on normal science procedure ensures the peculiar fact that to study anything like dramatic change of that society is literally unscientific. It steps outside the bounds specified by the procedures—

bounds that are closely policed by leading economists, most of whom have close association with liberal governments.

How can a science that is so policy-oriented manage to maintain the fiction of value-neutrality? The positivist methodology lies deep in economics and was a major factor in the postwar formalist revolution. Perhaps it was quite reasonable to give it a try, to see if the new techniques would indeed put economics into the status of a stable-law discipline. But whatever the motivations of recent practitioners, the value problem in economics is much older than that. Economics has been a liberal science for at least one century (since Marshall and Walras) and probably for two (since Smith). The real point does not seem to have been to make economics value-neutral in the large, for the subject is already committed beyond redemption there. Instead it has been to make economic science as value-neutral as possible in the small, and simply inoperative in the large. To be useful as a policy science within the established framework of society, it must be possible to use the discipline to discuss the marginal adjustments that are being contemplated by various decisionmakers in society. This requires a property that might be called value-communicability, the structuring of issues in a way that does not hopelessly distort the properties of alternatives from the point of view of the established participants. Economics seems to do this very well. But big issues cannot be discussed in economics, and probably no more strikingly "scientific" means of regulating the discipline in this socially functional way could be imagined than that provided by the formalist revolution. It literally killed two birds with one stone.

Even so, the problems that economics faces today may well be inconsistent with that serenely progressing normal science. Velikovsky has reared his head once more, the structure of society is changing sharply, and in contrast with the Keynesian case, this time unfavorably for the mainline profession. The new discipline, in order to deal with problems of detail, has had to make some real-world commitments, and it is in precisely these areas—policy macroeconomics, externality microeconomics, etc.—that it is failing to deliver the intellectual goods, even in the small.

Part II

Marxism

4

Marxist Economics as a Science

Probably only a few readers were troubled by the fact that something called "economics" was discussed in Part I without any mention of Marxism. Particularly for a British or American reader, this is perfectly natural usage. But Marxism has been around for as long as neoclassical economics; in fact, Marx published major works before either Marshall or Walras. With the years Marxism has not declined but grown in the number of its adherents, and also in the number of people who call themselves both economists and Marxists and who are products of professional programs of Marxist economic education. Marxist economists do talk and write about the economy. So the question arises as to the connections between the last section's topic and Marxist economics. Given the prevalent attitudes toward Marxism among neoclassical economists, the first order of business will be to appraise the extent to which Marxist economics can make good on its claim to being scientific. Is Marxist economics a science in Kuhn's sense?

Puzzles

If Marxism is to qualify as a Kuhnian science, perhaps the principal test it must pass is the possession of a set of puzzles that define the ways in which economic problems are to be analyzed. These puzzles do exist, all right, or perhaps one should speak not so much of puzzles as of puzzle-forms—of types of puzzles that can be applied fairly generally to whole classes of problems. There are at least three of these which are quite well developed within the Marxian tradition.

The first and classic puzzle of Marxism is defined by the question: How can there be exploitation when goods exchange at their labor-values? Marx's answer to this question lies right at the heart of Marxism: the worker receives for his labor only enough to ensure his survival plus enough to rear a replacement: the labor-value of his labor. Any labor-time he provides the entrepreneur beyond this, increases the labor-value of the product, but not the worker's own income. This is the opportunity that the capitalist exploits. The simplicity of the answer, and the powerful and plausible imagery of exploitation it evokes in many readers, may well be a principal factor in Marxism's survival. It is the puzzle whose solution distinguishes Marxism from classical economics as codified in Ricardo.

The usual neoclassical response to the labor theory of value is one of curt dismissal, on the grounds that the neoclassical theory of relative prices provides a far more accurate and satisfying theory of value than the labor-value theory, and was indeed designed as a reaction to the latter theory. This is quite true, but it misses the essential point, which is that labor-value supports a theory of distribution, while neoclassical price-theory does not, or at least not one with which even neoclassical economists feel very comfortable. In this Marxist puzzle, labor-value is a stylized fact, serving to concentrate attention on the process of capitalist distribution; the fact that it is not an ideal theory of relative prices may not be particularly relevant. This depends on whether one gets in trouble with the assumption, when thinking about distribution. Also, it should be remembered that labor-value has not entirely disappeared from neoclassical economics as an occasionally used stylized fact, as some input-output and production studies suggest.[1]

There are two rather different types of application of this puzzle-form that suggest its range of applicability. The first may be called the socialist-opportunity-cost version and follows Marx's own analysis in the Critique of the Gotha Program. The notion here is that not all the difference between the cost of reproduction of the laborer and the labor-value of his product should be counted as exploitation, because some part of it goes to investment in industries producing goods consumed by workers. Even some portion of the cost of government may be included as common to both socialist and capitalist societies. In this way the rate of exploitation must be modified to take account of those costs of maintaining the rate of production of necessary goods which are unavoidable regardless of the social form of organization of society.

This was not really a central question for Marx, whose stage theory suggested that socialism would come with higher technology, thus making comparisons based on the same technology irrelevant. Marx and most Marxists concentrated on the absolute size of the surplus. Whether they would have been more persuasive among the workers with a more sophisticated version is not a question of interest to us; the point here is that this puzzle-form is capable of generating additional puzzles which can occupy the serious attention of Marxist scholars via comparisons of estimates of the rate of exploitation in various times and places and the explanation of variations.

A second interpretation of the exploitation puzzle might be called the fate-control version. In 'it, power and alienation are related. One is interested in the extent to which each of the social classes is able to control its social environment. The argument is that control of the economy, and especially of the surplus it produces, is the appropriate measure of that control. The rate of exploitation is measured by the portion of the product whose distribution is taken from the control of the workers and handed over to the various economic and political agencies of the capitalist class for divvying up. Even though some resources are allocated from the surplus for investment in wage-goods industries, this is not a plus for the worker because of his lack of control over the distribution process, and also because of the distortions that control entails even for apparently benevolent allocations (for example, is the investment being used to buy off a segment of the working class that is threatening to become militant?).

A second puzzle-form goes as follows: How can progress beget not more progress but catastrophe? This one, too, does not have a significant counterpart in neoclassical economics. The equilibrium notion does not naturally invite discussions of progress, and neoclassical dynamics is usually formulated in models in which reasonably rational behavior on the part of the relevant agents will assure steady progress, in the sense of increasing per capita output, for the indefinite future. There is a strain of pessimism in the liberal tradition that has occasionally manifested itself, especially in the more conservative versions of neoclassical economics, but there, too, the problem is more often than not formulated in ways which make progress at least feasible, if one can only figure out what progress is.

The Marxian notion of progress breeding collapse is centered in the stage theory, and especially in the notion that there is a within-stage dynamic which first promotes progress but then begins to turn against itself, so to speak, and forces the economy and society down toward a crisis out of which the next social stage is born. The only stage thoroughly analyzed by Marxists in these terms is capitalism, but here the possibilities for developing "krakh" or collapse theories are legion. For example, there are numerous ways in which dynamic models can be made to reveal this phenomenon. In traditional Marxist approaches, cycles of steadily increasing amplitude served as the primary mode of explication. More promising these days would be a model in which there are boundary conditions whose penetration by increasing values of one variable generates a dramatic change of behavior among others, including reversals in the direction of movement. The exploration of some such models might provide some insights into plausible mechanisms of structural change and would be manifestations of the application of the krakh puzzle-form.

Neoclassical models are not entirely without some krakh properties themselves. There is at least one macro-model (not empirically estimated) in which, as the economy moves out of a recession toward full employment, the direction of impact (sign) of the multiplier suddenly changes. In others the model remains stable only because "safe" parameter values have been estimated. The whole procedure of model-building and model-testing in macroeconomics is biased toward building this sort of stable progress into the models. There is plenty to do within the second Marxist puzzle-form in reformulating old models and generating new ones that are designed seriously to get at the assumption of progress rather than accepting it as a sort of stylized fact.

The third puzzle-form asks the question: How can society simultaneously produce increasing affluence and increasing immiseration? There is a clear relation between this and the preceding puzzle-form, but historically the two have taken different turns, and in fact each grows out of a different aspect of Marx's work. The basic notion here has its origin in the "early Marx" notion of alienation as being destructive of the personality. It has not played a role in the history of orthodox Marxism, at least not until very recently. But in recent years the notion of alienation as more than counteracting the apparent benefits of higher consumption levels has become the centerpiece of analysis in the works of many socialist humanists and of Herbert Marcuse. There is much potential here for additional effort; indeed, the conceptual groundwork for serious empirical investigation of the theory has yet to be laid.

These three puzzle-forms are not exhaustive for Marxist economics, but they cover a wide range of topics, and one or another of them plays a role in analyses of such varying phenomena as the imperialist distortion of developing countries, the preservation of political stability in developed capitalist societies, and the effect of increasing monopoly on capitalism. They indicate the capability of Marxism to support a scientific economics in terms of a reasonably well-defined and potentially self-sustaining set of puzzles.

Framework

The intellectual framework within which Marxists work is quite explicitly stated in most standard works. The problem is rather the reverse: Many authors identify themselves as Marxists but then drop some key features of the framework without explanation or analysis. We are concerned here not to restate the framework but to comment briefly on a few of its elements, whether authors typically leave them in or out, that are most relevant for research in Marxist economics.

The dialectic is one of those aspects of Marxism to which authors most frequently feel compelled to pay lip service without actually using. In practice, what usually remains of the dialectic is not a form of world-historical logic but an implicit theory of stability. Rarely does one find Marxist economists genuinely arguing within the frame of the Hegelian triads of thesis-antithesis-synthesis, negation of the negation, and transformation of quantity into quality; indeed Marx himself was not fully at home in their use. However, forces in society are often claimed to be in a state of dialectic tension. By this, authors seem to mean two things: first, that the balance of forces is not stable, so that relatively small changes in the environment may precipitate large changes in social states; second, that the situation is open-ended in the sense that any of a number of factors may be the precipitant of the next round of changes. Thus Baran, in arguing the case for the crisis of monopoly capitalism, recognizes that in the shortrun the balance of forces permits more or less steady-state growth of capitalist society. His analysis centers around the forces which are building up during this process through the growing misuse of the growing surplus. The tension need not be manifested in any dramatic shifts in the variables in equilibrium. What is growing, along with the surplus, is instability—the steadily narrowing range of displacements from which the system has the ability to return to equilibrium or steady-state growth. So, the system is approaching the state of dialectic tension defined above.

But there is more to the dialectic than this. Neither quite a theory about the behavior of society, nor quite a logic, it is a tendency in thought, something that most Marxists identifiably have in common when they look at a problem and that helps define the range of acceptable solutions to puzzles. This tendency has four main components which can perhaps best be expressed by slogans: 1) not harmony but conflict; 2) not equilibrium but change; 3) not Platonic Truth, but forms of understanding that change with society; 4) not autonomous social sciences, but the integrated science of society. The typical social pattern, it is implied, is one in which conflict is developing, moving toward some crisis whose resolution will change both society and the ways men view their world. Of course the movement may be interrupted at times by periods of stasis, or may be difficult to observe for various reasons, and it is at this point that the dialectic tends to assume the more explicit form of the above paragraph.

Baran's thesis on the movement of monopoly capitalism shows these tendencies in operation. Class conflict remains at the heart of the model, though some of it is transmuted into conflict between a large segment of developed capitalist society, including some portion of the workers, and the Third World peoples [1]. Growth is essential to the survival of capitalist society in order to continue to increase employment with the growth of the labor force, but through the increasing waste which is the only socially feasible way of dealing with the ever-growing surplus, the nature of growth is changing in quality [2]. This process can continue for some time without apparent destructive consequences, but as consciousness of the effect of the process grows, resistance will also be bound to increase, though the early effects may involve no more than the growth of alienation [3]. The state plays a central role in the process of increasing the surplus, and this relative increase in government size, rather than the application of Keynesian economics, is the principal contribution of government to further capitalist development [4]. This capsuled argument uses the four tendencies in order and implies overall the stasis-instability thesis.

Two other elements in the Marxist framework are worth a brief comment. The class variable is of course indispensable for a Marxist. However, the issue was treated by Marx rather more subtly than by many of his followers. For Marx the basic conflict was indeed between those who owned the means of production and those who did not. But during many periods in the history of capitalism, center stage is held by segments within the bourgeoisie who are struggling to increase their respective shares of the surplus. Only when a serious threat from below manifests itself does the bourgeoisie close ranks in opposition, thereby revealing clearly the elemental force of class conflict.[2] Despite the crudities of some of Marx's followers, there is ample reason to treat this more developed theory of class conflict as a part of the Marxist tradition.[3]

The surplus poses a more serious problem. Generally discussions of surplus and the related term, waste, are dismissed by neoclassical economists as being unscientific, because the terms cannot be defined without bringing in the writer's value-judgments: "One man's waste is another man's nectar." There is no denying the criticism: the concept of the surplus is inextricably tied to the question as to what is necessary to a society and what is not. In Marx's own analysis, necessity is itself a social question, varying with time and place, which only serves to emphasize the value component. A central ingredient of Marxism is pushed into the foreground by this feature of the surplus: the belief that values can be objectively determined, so that words like "correct" and "incorrect" can be applied to them as the result of scientific analysis. Perhaps in no other area do the official methodologies of neoclassical and Marxist economics differ more than here.

Issues

As an example of the way in which issues become transformed as they move from the public arena to the special publics of neoclassical and Marxist economists we may take the case of turn-of-the-century discussions of international interaction. The public discussion dealt with questions such as the Boer War and the rising tide of international economic competition. These were transformed by neoclassical economics into discussions of tariff policy, protectionism versus free trade, the study of capital flows, and the effects on the international monetary mechanism. In this way the problems were turned into policy issues of the sort that politicians in the developed countries had to face, though often stylized by the special professional orientation of the neoclassical economist. For Marxists, however, the problem was to interpret these events in terms of the longer-run movement of capitalism, with special attention to modes of exploitation and the threat of capitalist collapse. The theory of imperialism was the major outgrowth of this in Marxist literature, together with the closely related theories of monopoly capitalism and of the role of banking and finance in the changing mode of capitalist operation.[4]

It is sometimes argued that neoclassical economics is too abstract, or alternatively too concerned with relatively trivial problems, to be relevant to contemporary issues; it is sometimes also argued that Marxism operates at a level too general and vague to provide any real guidance to contemporary problems. Both these positions are in a certain sense incorrect. In each case the puzzles and intellectual framework of the two orientations govern the way in which practitioners look at problems, and consequently at the detail of analysis that is employed and the extent to which broader-gauge factors are introduced. The world is analyzed differently depending on what you plan to do with it.

The Invisible College and Power

Vast numbers of serious Marxist journals appear all over the world, and many are devoted primarily to economic problems. But the eager reader, fresh from a perusal of the classics, who delves into these journals in order to see how Marxist science has developed during the twentieth century, is in for a major disappointment. Far from exhibiting the analysis of problems of detail that one expects from a normal science, far from exploring the ramifications of the theory left in so unfinished a state by Marx and Engels, these journals are mostly devoted to journalistic accounts of contemporary events, nitpicking discussions of essentially definitional matters, and reviews and polemics on the works of Marxists and neoclassicals. With only occasional exceptions, Marxism comes across in the journal literature as an ideology, not a science.

By the "lower-limit" standards of Chapter 1, there were perhaps fewer than twenty Marxist economists in the world around 1960; that is, fewer than twenty competent and productive economists working more or less full-time, seriously attempting to solve economic puzzles within the Marxian framework. None of these was residing in the Soviet Union.[5] Perhaps a comparable number was active twenty years earlier. It is possible that the number actively at work has increased substantially since, but the fruits of their work have hardly begun to appear.

Some of this is easily explained. Marxist writers living in socialist countries are not free to follow one of Kuhn's basic rules of science: that only the judgment of colleagues is accepted as relevant in defining problems and solutions. Changes in Marxist dogma must be approved by political authorities before economists can be expected to use them, or in many cases even to discuss them freely. Even in that most liberal of socialist countries, Yugoslavia, where some highly creative Marxist writing has in fact occurred, there have been a number of *de facto* constraints on the "normal" development of Marxist economics. In all other socialist countries the constraints on the invisible college are substantially greater.

In the West, too, there are constraints, though of a different sort. The leading Communist parties have close ties with one or another of the socialist countries, so that intellectuals affiliated with one of these parties are subject to similar, if weaker on the average, constraints to those of their colleagues farther east.

But many Marxist economists are subject to neither of these constraints, and still the normal development of Marxism has not occurred. This seems to be partly a matter of self-restraint; writing in a country whose régime and media are hostile, the Marxist seems often to feel constrained to pull his punches, to defend the faith in order to avoid the misunderstandings that may result from the inevitable controversy that accompanies the normal development of a science. Another factor is the tendency for even the more scholarly Marxist economists to turn Marxism into a set of political slogans to be used in an attempt to sway the masses rather than to develop a more secure understanding of the forces at work in modern society.

One of the greatest failings of twentieth-century Marxism was its inability to transcend nationalism. We need not list the reasons for this, but a consequence was the reinforcement of the divisive tendencies inherent in the breakup of the potential invisible college into a set of schools whose conflict is not basically over the scientific interpretation of Marxist economics, but over power in the wider world. Given the revolutionary aims implicit in Marxist thought, a certain amount of this was inevitable, but there has been so much of it that there have been basic failures in the ability of Marxist economics, as articulated by its twentieth-century proponents, to deal persuasively with many aspects of modern economic life.

In summary, Marxism passes most of the tests necessary for a Marxist economic science to exist in the Kuhnian sense, but in practice has failed because of the virtual absence of an integrated social system of scientists oriented toward the systematic development of the science through study of problems of detail. It has the puzzles and the network of commitments sufficient to develop as a science, but in fact its development has been distorted and spotty.

5

Twentieth-Century Marxism

If Marxism is a Kuhnian science, it is an early science, in which rival schools flourish and first principles continue to be argued at least as frequently as problems of detailed development. This, I think, is the clear result of a straightforward application of Kuhn's tests for a normal science to Marxist economics. But perhaps there are inherent reasons why sciences of society should differ from the natural sciences that form the basis of Kuhn's appraisal. Two such reasons seem particularly relevant.

The first of these is essentially political or ideological. Because economists are studying, among others, themselves, there are some difficulties in truth-seeking by means of normal science that are greater than for most natural sciences. The requirement—and it *is* necessary to the functioning of normal science—that the practitioners share a "network of commitments," opens the door to the use of ideologies for screening purposes in a social science. The underlying ideological commitment can even be used as a substitute, though not a perfect one, for the arbitration by fact that is supposedly the hallmark of a science. We have seen that the tendency in contemporary economics toward definition of puzzles more in terms of procedures than results can support such a substitution, and in fact probably has done so.

Marxist economists, of course, possess their own ideology. Despite their fragmentation, they do share a number of beliefs, the most important of which is their orientation toward those whose economic position deprives them of significant power to control their social destinies; at least this is true in capitalist countries. Marxism serves as a sort of counterscience to the status quo–oriented neoclassical economics. Its function, like that of colleagues in the invisible college, is to pick up on the weak links in the assumptions and arguments of the opposing system of thought and to develop alternatives within the counterideology. One is not surprised to find some fragmentation, for there are various kinds of have-nots in society, and when one such group acquires intellectual defense it is likely to have some unique features; also, the resources available to the have-nots do not permit the same scale of operation as for the neoclassical economists.

The second reason supporting some special features for a social science stems from the Velikovskyan nature of the object of study. The scientific laws of society, and especially of economics, change from time to time with such things as technology, social and political structure, and changes in the natural environment, as previously argued. Some such change is going on all the time, and sets upper limits to the amount that can be learned about the functioning of the economy. So, beyond a certain point, normal science study of social phenomena will be merely spinning its gears, generating studies without improving understanding. In this environment a sort of global search mechanism which emphasizes interaction between economics and the factors mentioned above, may often be a superior truth-seeking process. So in this sense, too, some basic deficiencies of Marxism as a normal science may be justified as contributing to understanding rather than the reverse. Whether that is what Marxism has actually done is a question of fact, and a brief sketch of twentieth-century Marxism will offer some parts of an answer to the question.

From Creativity to Stagnation

Twentieth-century Marxism has had a roller-coaster career. The immediate successors of Marx and Engels developed the science in three main directions: the study of imperialism, of monopoly capitalism, and of revisionism, that is, of the evolutionary development of capitalism toward socialism. Especially during the first two decades of the century, there was very lively discussion of many issues relating to the structure and movement of capitalism, particularly in the German and Russian language areas. Much of it looked like early-science attempts to get straight on basic elements of the framework and puzzles. For example, Hilferding's thesis about the role of investment banks in controlling the German economy could not be transferred to the British environment without some modification, because investment banks were not of central importance to the British economy, and this in turn was prerequisite to the success of analyses of imperialism in terms of joint action by monopoly capitalists in the developed countries. This was essentially the form in which one of the Marxist puzzles went into World War I. It was a puzzle in the sense that Marxists were confident it could be resolved, but did not yet have agreement as to how. But it was more than a normal science puzzle in that rather fundamental aspects of Marxism were at issue. If monopoly capitalism was evolving in different ways in different countries, the outcomes too might be different. That would require a good deal more modification of Marx than if the differences among advanced capitalist countries were largely epiphenomenal, and a more complex theory would be needed to generate the prediction of a coming general crisis.

Imperialism too possessed its puzzles. For example, Rosa Luxemburg argued that the prime mover for imperialist expansion was the search for markets in an environment in which each region of the world had an upper limit to its capacity to absorb capitalist production, an upper limit already reached in most regions within the advanced countries. For others it was not stagnating but expanding capitalist production that created imperialism, with the leading countries engaged in a keenly competitive search for raw materials to feed their expanding factories. This puzzle, too, was unresolved by World War I, and it also clearly had fundamental consequences for Marxist theory, as would any controversy pitting stagnationists against expansionists.

These puzzles were not resolved during the interwar period. Instead Marxism itself stagnated, at least as a theory of the functioning of capitalist society. Here and there a few important studies appeared, such as Sternberg's and Hallgarten's studies of imperialism, Dobb's study of the transition from feudalism to capitalism, and Sweezy's codification of Marxian value theory. But all in all, it was a very disappointing harvest, considering the expectations that the seeding of the earlier period would legitimately allow.[1] There were probably two principal reasons for this. The first has already been mentioned: the political suppression and self-restraint that the existence of the Soviet Union exercised on a great many Marxists. But most Marxist economists outside the Soviet Union were not members of the Communist party. To understand their intellectual stagnation as Marxists, we must turn to the third of the major developments of Marxism in the earlier period—to revisionism.

The founder of revisionism, Edouard Bernstein, argued essentially that the progress-breeds-catastrophe puzzle was a false one, that the recent history of Germany especially showed that progress was breeding more progress, even by socialist standards. Through this door the established Social Democratic politicians were glad to walk, though for political reasons they could not change their rhetoric as much as their behavior. After World War I, when the Social Democrats, stripped by the war of many of their most dynamic younger cadres, found themselves holding the reins of government in Germany, it was still more natural for them to believe the revisionist interpretation. But the issues they now faced had suddenly been transformed into the same form as those faced by rulers in the other advanced capitalist countries. They no longer required a revolutionary's understanding of how society worked and how it failed; they needed the active policy-maker's understanding. Evolutionary orientation only reinforced this view: the way to improve society was to move it along step by step in the right direction. Marxist economists who were associated with the Social Democratic party felt this too, and were not so very slow to recognize that neoclassical economics offered some of the answers to their problems. The history of revisionism is essentially a history of the conversion of Marxist economists to the neoclassical persuasion. Thus their "stagnation" was not that at all, but a shift to a different mode of analysis which was better suited to their new concerns.

However, there was one part of the world where Marxist economists were responding creatively, as Marxists, to their new environment: the Soviet Union. Here the exciting job of designing a new socialist society and getting it to work had to be faced, and quite a number of Marxist economists were in place and eager to contribute to the understanding of the problem. Furthermore, the political environment was relatively favorable for the flowering of their work. Various orientations toward the economy were permissible so long as they possessed some political support in the upper echelons of the party, and a great variety of positions was in fact represented among economists of the period.

Perhaps only in Cambridge, England, was there as stimulating and creative an effort to develop economics underway during the 20's. Many of the guiding ideas of the formalist revolution were articulated, or at least foreshadowed during that time. Modern growth theory, input-output analysis, problems of shortrun control of the economy in terms of sectoral instrument variables, the problem of balance between industry and agriculture during the development process, agricultural supply-response, and a number of other modern (neoclassical) puzzles were formulated more or less explicitly and argued in the same terms. Mathematics was a fairly commonly applied tool, and the analysis of masses of statistical data was under very rapid development. Indeed, when perusing the key works of the period, one has the feeling of reading a flawed and somewhat crabbed draft of a proposed contemporary textbook in economic planning and development.[2]

It should have been a tremendously exciting experience for a competent neoclassical economist to have read that draft, say, around 1930. But unfortunately it was not to be. Neoclassical economists did not read Russian, some of the most interesting papers used mathematics which put them beyond the reach of most neoclassicals of the time, and most important of all, neoclassical economists did not seriously read the works of Marxists in any language. Perhaps, even so, some of these ideas would have quickly percolated to the West in the 30's, but Stalin suppressed almost the entire group of participants in these great debates, and their accomplishments disappeared from view for almost three decades.

Renaissance?

Between 1956 and 1964 four major works of Marxist economics appeared—works which suggest that there is a good deal more life in Marxism than the last section might indicate. They are: Paul Baran's *The Political Economy of Growth,* Ernest Mandel's *Marxist Economic Theory,* Branko

Horvat's *Toward a Theory of Planned Economy,* and Herbert Marcuse's *One Dimensional Man.*[3] The first of these years witnessed the Polish October and the Hungarian revolution, marking a sort of nadir in the worldwide repute of Marxism. But then the Algerian revolution was brought to a successful conclusion, the Cuban revolution and the Chinese Great Leap occurred, and the student revolt in the western world began to be felt. The genesis of these works seems to be largely independent of the great events of the time, but for whatever reason the dramatic change in the fortunes of Marxism as an ideology occurred at about the same time as its intellectual reawakening.

Of the four authors, two—Baran and Marcuse—were resident in the United States at the time they published the relevant books, while Mandel was Belgian and Horvat a Yugoslav; significantly, however, none of these men received their formal education in the United States.[4] Marxism remains a Continental phenomenon. Each of their works is a broad synthetic effort and in no sense a detailed contribution to the development of a Marxian normal science. Instead, each work may best be considered an attempt to change the general course of Marxism in a particular direction; and each direction is quite different from the others.

Only a few indications of the significance and tenor of these works will be given here, but hopefully enough to make the case for a possible reawakening plausible. Despite their quite fundamental differences, all four writers are Marxists in the sense that the framework of class and exploitation remains at the center of the study of capitalist society, and all quite explicitly intermingle various anticapitalist value-judgments with their facts.

Of the four writers, Mandel is closest to some sort of mainline trajectory of Marxist thought. His chief aim is to reestablish the Marxian framework by rewriting the general Marxian theory of social movement, taking account of the accumulated empirical evidence. Among his most interesting modifications is the dropping of the hoary five-stage schema of history for a much looser historical interpretation in which the two most dramatic structural changes come with the rise of cities and the rise of modern industry and technology. The progress-catastrophe puzzle-form plays little or no role in his analysis, the emphasis being on alienation and fate-control forms of analysis. Mandel's economic analysis is a little weak, and his reading seems to be relatively more comprehensive in sociology, but sociology is perhaps the best place in which to gain an understanding of the modern framework in social thought and the stylized facts with which most contemporary Marxist economists are likely to work.

Horvat's work in general outline resembles Mandel quite closely. Both treat the Soviet Union as an exploitative society, both are prepared to revise Marx where they feel it necessary, and both believe that worker control is the key to the next stage of social and economic progress. But Horvat has dual training both in Yugoslav Marxism and neoclassical economics, and the result of this is to introduce some neoclassical puzzles into his Marxist frame of reference. Horvat accepts the marginalist analysis as useful both for socialist planners and for worker-managed enterprises, and sees the market as playing a central role in socialist resource-allocation. In addition, he has a novel and striking theory of growth that argues, roughly speaking, that there is virtually no shortrun cost to be borne in terms of foregone consumption if a maximum-growth policy is adopted by a developing country. Indeed, Marxian puzzles are rather hard to find in Horvat; for example, his structural transformations tend to occur because the new form is recognized as superior to the old, thereby creating social pressures for the reform, and inefficiency rather than alienation seems to play the central role in determining the relative superiority of alternative social structures. Nevertheless, Horvat represents a serious attempt at melding the two traditions, and his Marxism is also well developed, especially in the macrohistory sections of his work.

Baran's work is, like Mandel's, more in the orthodox tradition, but as an economist Baran is more concerned to develop the analysis of major contemporary problems than to refurbish the framework of analysis. His theory of imperialism puts greater emphasis on two factors than is quite traditional: the destruction of the social fabric of "developing" countries, long before modern economic development began, by various types of incursions from the economically advanced nations; and the consequent political devices by which these nations are able to keep the developing countries in economic thrall. This is a straightforward application of the exploitation puzzle, the novelty lying in the special analysis of the initial conditions in which modern economic exploitation begins, and the more sophisticated treatment of the instruments available to capitalists from the advanced nations and their governments. In the discussion of monopoly capitalism, Baran reformulates the concept of surplus and analyzes the movement of monopoly capitalist countries in terms of the processes generating waste of the surplus in a situation of increasing lack of sufficient real investment opportunities.

Baran seems a little uneasy with the alienation argument and interprets the trend of increasing waste as a progress-castastrophe phenomenon, though without any analysis of the process of collapse.

Finally there is Marcuse, who, though trained as a philosopher, has written a book that must be considered a major contribution to Marxist economic thought. Marcuse has pushed both technological determinism and subjective analysis of alienation to a much greater extent than the other writers. Technology generates affluence in a neat plastic-and-chrome atmosphere where man's appetites are all subject to instant satisfaction, his personality fragmented, his alienation so distorting his nature that he comes to identify with his alienated state, to achieve a superficial and soul-destroying "happy consciousness." There is no progress-catastrophe syndrome built into this system; those who have been given the full socialization treatment are effectively emasculated. Hence structural transformation, if it comes, will be the result of an alliance among those who have not yet been "treated" for the disease of nonmodernity. Marcuse works entirely with the affluence-immiseration puzzle-form, and though he sees exploitation and even the possibility of catastrophe breeding change, these are not subjects of analysis.

It is probably true that there is a wider range of disagreement among these authors over the nature of the good socialist society than there is over the nature of capitalism. Nevertheless there are important differences both of substance and of orientation with respect to the causal factors underlying capitalism's change, particularly with respect to the role of consciousness. Baran and Horvat are the most "conservative" on this dimension, for despite Baran's discussion of waste he takes material output per capita as a good measure of economic performance, and Horvat uses a similar measure. Marcuse lies at the opposite extreme; one might characterize his view of individual commodities as implying that they take their value from the social environment within which they are embedded, so that conventional measures of output are largely meaningless. Mandel is somewhere in between. This by no means exhaustive list of differences suggests that if Marxism has reawakened it has also stepped immediately into a crisis.

The development of Soviet economics during the 60's is often referred to as a renaissance; however, few writers using this term have Marxism in mind. For example, this blossoming did not build on the suppressed work of Soviet writers of the 20's. Instead, the new intellectual masters of Soviet economics were western neoclassical economists, the leaders of the formalist revolution. Of particular interest in the main Soviet writings were the new techniques of planning that had been developed and applied extensively, if not first invented, in the West. Such things as linear programming and input-output analysis became topics of central interest to the younger and intellectually most active men and women in the field. Degree programs were started in mathematical economics at major universities, and books, articles, even a new major journal, cemented the professional relations among the new breed of economists. It looked very much like a scientific revolution within Soviet economics.

But borrowing from the West did not stop with a few techniques of quantitative analysis suitable for use in the actual practice of economic planning. The book that aroused the most public comment as the bellwether of change, written by the mathematician Kantorovich,[5] presents a sort of vision of a reformed socialist society in which institutions are adapted so as to make the price system function effectively. Theoretical ideas with no direct practical applicability were transferred intact to the Soviet scene, and such strange phenomena appear as formal analyses by official Marxist economists of infinite streams of utility, measured in cardinal units very like those that might have been employed by some anti-Marxist Austrian School economist of eighty years ago.

Still further, the new discipline was only well underway when advocacy of reform began to reach the policy level. Economists, many of them closely associated with the new school of thought, began to argue that the incentive system of the production sector should be based on prices which were also to serve the role of determining the opportunity costs of all participants in decision-making. In some areas, especially agriculture, the advocacy went to the point of proposing the use of an ordinary market system. The student of these developments finds it hard to escape the conclusion that Soviet economists have taken over a good deal more than a set of value-neutral techniques from the West; a fair part of the network of commitments of neoclassical economists seems to have been sucked in along with the mother's milk of formalist economics.

The economists and their putative allies among other groups of intellectuals did not have the power to get these liberal reforms put into practice in the Soviet Union, and their political activity seems to have tapered off from a sort of peak reached in the early sixties. But within the discipline, the school is in the process of taking over Soviet economics, and perhaps they have already reached the stage at which the applied workers among them are indispensable, so that many would at least personally survive any "ordinary" purge. But once again the question posed by the history of revisionism is raised: Doesn't neoclassical economics have such a broad range of applicability that it can survive any scientifically fair competition with Marxism? Recent Soviet history provides further evidence of crisis in Marxist economics.

Finally, one might note some mild stirrings among the official Soviet Marxists who during most of this period have continued to grind out their parodies of Marxist economic science. Here and there, especially in politically less sensitive areas, a somewhat deeper empirical content can be found mixed in with the polemics. Partly this is a product of the significant thaw of the last fifteen years, which among other things has permitted a fair number of Soviet students of capitalist countries to actually visit those countries. Perhaps it is partly also due to some recognition of the inevitable interaction between Soviet Marxism and the new Soviet economics, and of the need for the former to acquire some modicum of intellectual respectability if it is to survive that interaction. Thus the relation between Marxist and neoclassical economics is rapidly coming to assume the same shape in the Soviet Union as it has in the West, though Marxism is still well protected by the state against the crisis of fundamental challenge within the field that western Marxism is facing.

Marxism in Crisis?

The problem posed by the interpenetration of neoclassical and Marxist analysis might be resolved by some sort of integration of the two. This view is typically held by younger radical economists in the United States; it is the approach taken by Horvat. However it seems to me that this is a little too glib, for a variety of reasons. In the first place, the class bias in the two systems of thought lies heavily between them, permeates each thoroughly, and is probably not to be integrated by cutting and pasting; what would be required is a substantial change of world-view, a scientific revolution in Kuhn's sense. The strong technocratic bias in neoclassical economics is likely to be destructive of the values of a socialist society and to foster the pressures toward return to an élitist régime.

Furthermore, the Soviet experience is not just a case of technical dominance of neoclassical economics in dealing with status-quo or marginalist policy issues. There is the evidence that there is, causally speaking, a tie-in sale connecting liberal philosophy and liberal economics: buy either one and you get the other free. For Soviet economists too, marginalism is useful to their clients and larger issues are largely ignored. Only a thorough paradigm change can deal effectively with this value bias inherent in the formalist techniques. There really is no such thing as a value-neutral technique, because one always brings some sort of framework of interpretation to bear on it. All revolutions of thought in economics have had this feature of value relevance, and even techniques have undergone a change of interpretation in the process.

Finally, one should remember that the avowed purpose of Marxists is the creation of a solidary society: one in which men relate to one another directly without the depersonalizing mediations of the commodity system. To the extent that this is really a fundamental feature of a socialist society, the neoclassical price system loses its applicability. Direct interactions are inevitably externalities, and no proposition in neoclassical economics is more firmly established than the one that says price-based allocations generally point the wrong way when externalities are present. If socialism is achieved, much of neoclassical economics will perforce disappear.

Svetozar Stojanović, a Yugoslav Marxist philosopher, recently spoke of the crisis of Marxism, of its time of "spiritual poverty" [6] in the interwar period, and of the signs of renaissance:

> There are now increasing signs of recovery from the disaster brought about by an almost schizoid split. I am referring to the Janus-faced attitude of numerous Marxists: radically critical toward capitalism, they were at the same time apologists for socialism. There are now indications that this split is disappearing because it is being increasingly understood that Marxism must be a critique of *all* existing societies. . . . The main chance for essential innovations in Marxism lies now, in my opinion, in analysis and critical evaluation of the sociopolitical practice which passes as socialism.[7]

The central theme of this part has been that Stojanović's remarks apply to Marxist economics as well as to other aspects of Marxist analysis. There may not be an iron law of oligarchy, but history has shown all too clearly the existence of an iron tendency toward élitist systems of social control. Every society, every individual, who wishes to restrict or eliminate élitism, will be faced with a continuing struggle. In economics the intellectual lines are rather clearly drawn, with neoclassical economics serving the cause of efficient élitism and Marxism the only major contender in opposition. At the present time these two intellectual systems are both promising and in deep trouble.[8]

6

What's Wrong with Economics I

Neoclassical economics is a full-fledged normal science: it passes all the tests. Furthermore, it is an expanding science, in that the economist's techniques have been finding first-time applications in a number of areas in recent years. Still further, there is a process of integration underway. Under the rubric of behavioral science a common language, set of ideas, and battery of techniques is being set up with broad application, among others, in political science, social psychology, business administration, and Soviet economics.[1] If anything, this process has been accelerating lately. Economics is the very model of a modern major discipline.

And yet there are some problems which are serious enough to have created a malaise among an apparently increasing number of economists, especially the younger and more radical ones. At the same time that it is expanding economics seems to be suffering a shrinking crisis in which the standard puzzles and techniques become increasingly incapable of resolving the social problems which lie behind them, even though the studies themselves are becoming steadily "better" by the criteria of normal economics. Much of this is attributable to the fact that questions of distribution and externalities are becoming relatively more important, and these areas are not successfully developed in modern neoclassical economics. It is all too easy to say that these are inherently more difficult subjects, and that accounts for their present state. But it is also true that neoclassical economics has a strong class bias, that its techniques discourage the endogenous treatment of political and social factors, however important they may be to a particular issue, and that a positivist methodology prevents the serious discussion of values, which may be interpreted as a device for perpetuating existing value-prejudices.

Marxist economics is not subject to the same class bias as neoclassical economics. Its practitioners are compelled by its framework to take broad interactive views of issues, and values play a central and substantive role as elements in the puzzles and techniques of analysis. Also, externalities and distribution play a central role in Marxist theory. Thus Marxism appears as a strong candidate to replace the neoclassical paradigm as the appropriate science for analyzing economies. Furthermore, the discipline seems to be in the throes of a renaissance, of an upsurge in ideas and interest that has not been matched for nearly half a century.

However, Marxism, though it is a science, is a badly flawed one. Its development has been aborted by political oppression in a number of countries, socialist and capitalist alike. Its practitioners have had a tendency to concentrate on popularizations and slogans, aimed at shortrun political goals, to the detriment of keeping the subject up to date and developing in its analysis of the issues of the time. And at present a crisis of competing orientations, combined with the above two factors, pose what may well be a survival threat to the discipline.

One is tempted to sloganize: neoclassical economics is beginning to look like a case of techniques without relevance, Marxism of relevance without techniques. But that would be to ignore a really fundamental difference between the two disciplines: their class bias. The neoclassical orientation might be called a using-the-institutions policy-orientation, Marxism a changing-the-institutions policy-orientation. Roughly speaking, each *is*—or at least *was*—relevant for its assigned task; furthermore, the techniques that each employs have a certain plausibility. It is reasonable to expect that an orientation toward marginal adjustments of a system believed to be in some sort of reasonable approximation to equilibrium will require sharper, more precise tools than an orientation toward dramatic structural change.

There seems to be a sort of three-way tension among the functional specializations of Marxist and neoclassical economics, their implicit and explicit biases, and the problems posed for them by contemporary issues. Given their functionality, the demise of one of the disciplines as a result of "free competition in the scientific marketplace of ideas," even if that environment were attainable, is undesirable because each possesses a fundamental bias. The elimination of that bias, or its transformation, is not a scientific topic within the usual interpretation of neoclassical economics, however desirable it might seem, and most

Marxists are insufficiently free of political intervention in their work to be able seriously to undertake such a task, though it would be methodologically permissible within their discipline. Finally, neither discipline has performed strikingly well in developing an understanding of how the modern world works, and each may actually be moving away from the truth rather than toward it.[2]

How can these tensions be resolved? That gloomy subject, methodology, holds some of the clues. The nature of man, the productivity of verification procedures, and the role of values in social science, clearly relate to the problems we have been discussing. We turn to them now to see if there are not some alternative formulations available which offer better guidance to the future development of our understanding of the economy.

Part III

Social Man

7

Conversions not Decisions

The concept of the decision lies at the heart of economics today. This has always been true of microeconomics, where the decisions of consumers, entrepreneurs, and owners of factors of production have been analyzed. The connection is less direct but still strong in macroeconomics, where it is generally considered desirable to be able to rationalize all behavioral relations in terms of plausible models of decision-making by the relevant agents. Even in the verification process the decision has become important as the investigator's decision about the relation between data and hypothesis defines the format of analysis of the verification process, at least in one popular version. Finally, the approach is spreading, to political science especially, but also to social psychology. It is not too strong to say that behaviorism, based on the analysis of decisions, bids fair to become the integrated social science of the future.

The decision, as conceived in this body of literature,

consists in the choice by an agent, from among a number of alternative courses of action, of that alternative which scores highest according to some criterion supplied by the agent. This seems unexceptionable; indeed it can be interpreted to be tautological in that any conceivable human behavior can be rationalized in terms of this sort of decision. But in practice it is not tautological, and has been productive of positive results with respect to human behavior. These results are achieved usually by asserting that the criterion is a stable reflection of the preferences of the agent and that the alternatives have known properties which permit comeasurement among them in terms of the arguments of the criterion. A picture of the decision maker begins to emerge even from this quite abstract characterization.

The argument of the next three chapters can be stated simply: the decision model is seriously flawed because of the interaction that occurs between criterion and alternatives during the decision process, and which results in a high degree of interdependence among decisions. This defect is sufficiently fundamental that it probably cannot be corrected simply by occasionally introducing such interaction explicitly as a sort of ad hoc modification of the standard model. In defending the thesis, we start with a few examples and arguments designed to emphasize the importance of attitude-change in individuals and the importance of social factors in such change. In the next chapter we turn to some philosophical considerations, and in the final chapter of the section discuss some economic aspects of the problem.

Conversions

Churchman tells the story [1] of a successful management consultant who believes that there is no such thing as a business decision, even though supposedly he makes his living assisting businessmen in making decisions. The implication of the story is that the manager's attitudes during the decision process are insufficiently stable to permit the modeling of the activity as a decision in the above sense. In effect, the manager worries about the problem for a while, and then *he changes.* This little story, perhaps apocryphal, will serve as the model for what is meant by a conversion. It is a change of some kind in the attitude of the agent that occurs during the process of decisionmaking and that forms an integral part of that process.

There are several ways in which attitudes can change. One simple way is for new information to come to light. The agent discovers that some prospective purchases have hidden charges added on to the quoted price, and this information leads to a new purchase decision. New information can lead the agent to change his criterion of judgment also. For example, suppose he learns that changes in the level of unemployment as usually measured are not too closely correlated with changes in the economic condition of our poorest citizens. This could lead our agent to advocate the introduction of a more poverty-relevant variable into policy discussions regarding the appropriate level of activity for the economy.

Changes of this kind do not pose any direct threat to existing ways of looking at decisions. One might hope that there would be some development of the theory to make the insertion of new information a part of the problem, and in fact efforts along this line are already underway. But suppose that the new information has a wider impact. For example, suppose that our prospective purchaser infers from this new information that he is really beset on all sides by attempts to snooker him into unwise purchases by some mix of false and misleading information; the message doesn't change, but the conclusion he draws from it does, and this conclusion leads to a very broad revaluation of a great many decisions. Suppose that our economist-agent takes the new unemployment study not at its face value, but as evidence that the discipline he supposed was a value-neutral science is riddled with class bias, with all that that entails for his own future decisions. The new information has now gotten out of hand, producing ramifications with which the standard decision model is very poorly equipped to cope.

But ordinary factual information is not the only device by which attitudes are changed. People are often convinced by arguments that are without any testable factual content. Probably most neoclassical economists who adopted Keynesianism in the late 30's and 40's did so without knowledge of new factual information, but only because the arguments about what might be the case sounded convincing. Certainly there was no information becoming available at that time which could not be explained by the old theories. And of course, values too can be changed as the result of exhortation, unless the moralists and preachers of a hundred generations have been wasting their breath completely.

These matters will be discussed at somewhat greater length later on. At the moment the important point to note is the common element among these various types of changes of attitude, after the simplest cases. This element is the interdependence between the immediate decision and later decisions, the mediator being the general world-view of the agent. The more important this factor becomes, the less interesting is the analysis of the individual decision as the basic element in social behavior.

Economists have never really believed that "preferences are stable"—i.e., that individual attitudes toward their alternatives in the areas of consumption, work, and leisure do not change. As suggested earlier, this is more of a stylized fact: an assumption that may well be wrong but is convenient and, supposedly, does not usually cause any trouble. But I suspect that part of the support for this view comes from the belief of many economists that personality is stable, that substantial changes in attitudes are quite rare and so not of interest to economists. This is more than a stylized fact: it is part of the neoclassical economist's world-view. And it is false.

Personality may be defined as the "relatively persistent dispositional tendencies existing 'within' persons." These tendencies "are in the main acquired in the course of experience rather than being innately determined, and they are subject to alteration as a consequence of new experience." These quotes are taken from a survey of interactional personality theory,[2] an approach in which the role of the environment in personality development is given relatively greater emphasis than in some other schools of psychology. It is also true that most of the literature on personality change is oriented toward pathology, so that dramatic changes in the behavior of "normal" or "average" individuals is not yet much studied by psychologists.

Nevertheless, the body of evidence on personality change is quite impressive. Countless examples of dramatic changes in orientation and behavior have come from the therapeutic situation, which at the very least makes plausible the argument that people not subject to severe psychological disturbance can also undergo personality changes.

A second major body of literature that deals fundamentally with personality change is developmental psychology. No one doubts that the personality—in our definition—of children changes as they mature. In recent years the continuing personality development of adults has become a subject of study, and the indications are that very substantial change over the adult lifetime is the rule rather than the exception.[3]

Of course, not everything changes. Indeed, there are indications that certain tendencies in personality may be genetically determined. But at the moment we are not trying to set limits to the possibilities for personality change or even to characterize its main features, but only to argue that economics has been left well behind the times in its theory of the human personality. These changes, small and large, persistent and transient, are sufficiently frequent and far reaching and relevant for the study of behavior, including economic behavior, that they must be brought within the purview of economists.

Social Aspects of Attitude-Change

The framework or world-view that plays a central role in orienting the behavior of the individual is the most obvious social product that lies within a human being. The learning processes that generated the world-view are almost all social in the sense that it is the views of others that are being inculcated by the process. This is as true of things learned from isolated reading as it is of things learned directly in a group situation. The individual is thoroughly immersed in a social nexus; consequently it is not surprising that he can change in response to signals from that nexus. A few examples of well-known types of change are perhaps of some use in showing the sorts of things that can be found out about the general process of attitude-change.

One of the most interesting processes of attitude-change is cognitive dissonance. In a classic experiment a group is put through an extremely long and tedious set of tests in an experimental situation. Half of these subjects are then told that another group is to be put through the same set of tests, and that these new subjects must be told by the old subjects how much fun the tests are as a means of getting their cooperation. This is done. After a period of time the original subjects are all interviewed, and it is found that the control group retains its memories of tedium while the other half of the group now believes that the experiments were substantially less tedious than the control group. Furthermore, the subjects were paid varying monetary awards, and those who received low pay underwent a greater attitude-change than those who received higher pay. This suggests that commitment was an important factor in generating the attitude-change. A number of different experiments along this same line have been carried out with the same general result: the subjects' attitudes are changed as a consequence of committing themselves socially to a point of view different from the one they previously held.[4]

Cognitive dissonance might well have been called conditioned conation. One of the major achievements of the Gestalt school of psychology was to establish the ubiquity of conditioned perception. Viewers of op art have been well introduced to this phenomenon, and the Necker cube, reproduced on this page, is a good example. It consists of twelve line-segments though most people have a great deal of difficulty perceiving it as simply that. But the perception is not fixed even for those who perceive it as a cube. For example, if one sees the lower righthand facet as nearest the viewer, by concentrating his attention the

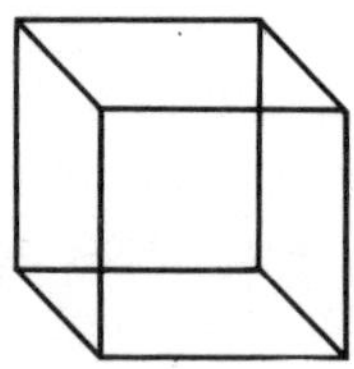

reader can switch perceptions, so that the upper lefthand facet suddenly becomes the nearest facet. With a little practice, the face of the cube can be made to pop in and out at will. In this example, what we see—our perceptions of the world around us—is being altered at will by changes in our internal state without any direct stimulus from outside. Or, as Hanson puts it, perception and interpretation are simultaneous (and interrelated).[5]

A still clearer demonstration of the social nature of much conditioning comes from an experiment with playing cards. The experimenter establishes minimum recognition-times for the subjects with respect to pictures of playing cards flashed on a screen. Then he begins inserting occasional ringers, such as a ten of spades that is colored

red as if it were a ten of hearts. The subjects, without hesitation, identify these cards as one or another of the regular cards. Exposure times are gradually increased until, after a considerable increase, some of the subjects begin to have doubts. These doubts and hesitations are finally resolved by the subject suddenly getting the idea that there may be ringers. After this is done no further difficulties are encountered in identification. However, some subjects are oppressed by considerable anxiety and occasionally are unable to recognize the ringers, even with very long exposure times. Kuhn used this experiment to exemplify the difficulties scientists encounter in facing anomalies or other challenges to central parts of their professional beliefs.[6]

Another striking example of social conditioning of perception comes from the history of art. Early artists in America were unable to perceive the wilderness. Its wild disorder was so different from the ordered beauty of the English countryside on which their perceptions and techniques were trained, that they could put no inkling of it on canvas for some years. In effect they imported their English eyes with them to the New World and were some time in growing new ones. In this case the social conditioning grew directly out of the social nature of their art, the training serving effectively to internalize the esthetic standards of the school to the point at which they seem actually to have seen things through the eyes of their own school.[7]

In the above examples we have concentrated on perceptual aspects of social conditioning, partly because there are a considerable number of examples at hand, but also because they seem to make the case for social conditioning quite strongly. If perceptions themselves can be so altered, it is not so difficult to credit comparable or even stronger changes in value-systems and belief-systems that do not rely so heavily on the "hard" data provided by the senses. Our aim is not to challenge the reality principle; quite the contrary, it plays the central role in the epistemology implicit in the views we are describing. Rather it is to show the range of phenomena that presently lie outside the economist's reach because of his attachment to old-fashioned notions.

Most of these examples have also dealt with relatively minor aspects of human behavior. I think they do, in combination with the literature that stands behind them, constitute a strong case for the frequency of conversions in human behavior. But there are still more significant conversions: those that affect a broad range of behaviors of the individual and of groups of individuals. Conversions of this kind can be divided into three groups which may be called cul-de-sac, indoctrination, and key-event conversions.

Cul-de-sac problems arise when individuals have, through a combination of events, got themselves into an intolerable situation as a result of behaving within some world-view. Given recognition that their attitudes are partly responsible for the predicament, the situation is favorable for the generation of a new set of attitudes. A model for this sort of personality change is Conrad's Lord Jim, whose cowardice leads to his ostracism, which in turns leads to a dramatic personality-change of which the performance of acts of prodigious bravery is but one aspect. A real-world example comes from the autobiography of Milovan Djilas. Twenty years ago this leader of the Yugoslav Communist party found his criticism of party members had produced in him a painful dilemma: either to continue the public criticisms and suffer a complete break with all his former friends and comrades in arms, including an inevitable prison sentence, or suppress the criticism and remain in the high party councils. A key telephone call in the middle of the night brought the dilemma to a head and produced an inward "tussle" over the choice. "But the tussle within me was short-lived; it lasted just a few minutes. . . . Because I already knew, yes *knew,* that this was my true self, and that I could not renounce it . . ." [8] Thus did Djilas "decide" on a course that was to cause his family great difficulties and put him in a usually unheated prison for many years. The speed of the "decision" is of course misleading: events and inward tussles had been preparing him for months for the moment. But this was no decision in the scientific sense of the word. It was an inward transformation which made the hard-nosed practitioner of the omelets-require-broken-eggs school of Communism into a violence-averse social democrat.

Each conversion is an individual affair in that an internal transformation of values is entailed. But mass conversions do occur. Every scientific revolution in the sense of Kuhn is such a mass conversion, in this case of scientists. Again, the most important elements in the process are likely to be not the immediate precipitants of a sudden conversion, but a series of events that gradually erodes confidence in old interpretations of the world and opens the mind to acceptance of some alternative. Also, conversions are probably not too often sudden and mystical in form, like that of St. Paul on the road to Damascus. The speed with which the process occurs is perhaps not too interesting; what counts is rather the extent of the change and the range of behaviors affected. For this class of conversions, the recognition that one has entered a cul-de-sac is the mind-opening event. Even then it is by no means certain that a conversion will occur. We are not presenting here a theory of the causes of conversions, merely trying to sensitize the reader to their importance for economics and for social science in general.

Indoctrination, the second type of conversion, occurs in many different ways. Perhaps the most widely quoted varieties occur in the socialization of the child within his family and at school. But we are more concerned with the indoctrination of adults. Training for a job or profession is probably the most widespread example. Kuhn's discussion of this indoctrination of scientists can be matched by training in such professions as law, medicine, and engineering, where the emphasis is not on scholarship but on the ability to carry out a particular kind of practical activity. Again development of favorable attitudes—and recruitment of favorable prospects—is an important part of the schooling, one of whose functions is to standardize the attitudes and reactions of the trainees to broad classes of situations.

One of the most extreme forms of indoctrination occurs in religious and military societies. The dozen years of preparation required of a Jesuit priest provides a striking example. Here an active attempt is made actually to induce a conversion experience in the trainee through a month-long retreat early in the training, and reports indicate rather frequent success. But such conversions need not be confined to the educated or professional. One of the more effective indoctrination procedures has been that carried out in the boot camps that provide initial training for enlistees into the Marine Corps. Many people have been impressed with the elements of transformation of character that have been brought about by this three-month program, which—like most such programs—completely isolates the trainee from his former contacts and lifestyle and assaults his body, mind, and spirit continually with the new attitudes and appropriate behaviors. There do not seem to be largescale tests of the consequences of this training, but the view is widespread that loyalty, obedience, skill, and attitudes toward risk and other aspects of behavior, are durably changed for a great many products of these regimens.[9]

Key events, the third type of conversion, are events which trigger attitude-changes without any element of deliberate design or without necessarily producing a cul-de-sac situation. For example, it has been found that a much-larger-than-chance proportion of doctors experienced a death in their families during childhood. The Great Depression was a more pervasive and durable event that seems to have had a profound effect on political attitudes in the United States. It was probably a trigger for the change in attitudes from self-help to welfare state, which is widely remarked as occurring in the mid-30's, was manifested politically in the 1936 election, and has been with us ever since. If true, this was a conversion for some millions, perhaps tens of millions of citizens, and converts continued to be created for years after that election.

8

Language and Change

One of the clichés of our time has it that the United States is playing Rome to Europe's Greece. There is considerable truth to this cliché. Intellectually speaking, the United States was still rather provincial in 1930. In the nineteenth century there were probably fewer great intellects in the United States than in Czarist Russia, and the derivative nature of our intellectual life was only beginning to change in a few fields by the onset of the Depression. Centering around the German-Jewish emigration of the 30's a new tradition was established, now known as the brain drain, by which American academia was able to use its vast resources to skim off a great deal of Europe's intellectual cream. This has been tremendously stimulating to the host institutions, but forty years later one is still struck by the high percentage of leading scholars in many fields who acquired their education, and with it many primary elements in their world-views, in Europe. The United States has become the research center of the world, but perhaps not the idea center.[1]

France provided the cultural home for the development of a number of the ideas of interest to us, as suggested by names like Lévi-Strauss, Piaget, Merleau-Ponty, and Camus, whose ideas have as yet had no impact on neoclassical economics. Their minimal impact on Marxism is probably explained by the "dinosaur" French Communist party, which has largely prevented the development of new ideas into an integrated left intellectual orientation.[2] Also, resources and institutions for the propagation and further development of new ideas are very weak in France. Had Nazism been avoided, the twentieth century would clearly have been Germany's century, intellectually speaking. As far as social science is concerned, many of the central ideas that have had substantial formative impact on social science in recent decades seem to have come out of the Germanic culture area, especially if one broadens the notion of German to include the culturally closely related Scandinavians and Dutch. The great formative ideas of existentialism, scientific methodology, and mathematical-statistical social science, are products largely of this part of the world.

But there is no profit in fighting old cultural battles. The point is that there is a Continental intellectual tradition, which has been tremendously creative, which has fed its new ideas—with varying time lags—into the semi-autonomous Anglo-American tradition, which has through emigrés exerted a very great influence on American higher education, but which seems hardly to have touched mainline economics. Neoclassical economics, the English science *par excellence,* has shown a powerful resistance to changes in its basic orientation. Even the formalist revolution, largely inspired from Continental research, was carried out in the United States, as we have seen, as a revolution of method far more than of substance.

But those ignored Continental ideas of the last generation or two cannot be held at bay indefinitely in a world as interdependent as ours. Even economists—the neoclassicals secure in their positions of power, the Marxists only somewhat less secure in their ideology—are beginning to be forced to come to terms with these ideas, to restructure their disciplines so that they can at least be seriously—that is professionally—discussed.

No attempt is made to survey these ideas in the few pages that follow. One or two are simply mentioned as being particularly pertinent for contemporary economics. Following our Roman tradition, we begin the exposition with a bit of technological discussion.

Whatever Became of Machine Translation?

The positivist conception of language was given a pretty good test in the machine-translation programs of the 50's. The positivist notion of a language had it consisting of a dictionary and a grammar. Each word has a meaning and can be combined with other words according to the rules of the grammar. The meaning of a string of words formed in this way was a function of the meanings of the individual words and their grammatical status. Though ordinary languages were recognized to be less orderly in structure than this, the theory was thought to be close enough to the truth to provide a good basis for computerized translation, especially of scientific texts where the consistency of language and structure should be highest.

Quite a lot of money and expert time was put into the effort of developing usable computer translations of scientific texts. There was a clear practical advantage to success, but there was also the opportunity to see how well this notion of what a language is, fit reality. The attempt was a decisive failure, and computer programs for serious translation work are today farther from realization than they were thought to be in the early 50's.[3] Languages, even those used by scientists to report on their research, are far more complicated than the positivist model allowed. Most important and fundamental of all was the failure attributable to the attempted separation of form and substance, of structure and meaning. Meaning turns out to be a function of context as well as of structure and the meaning of individual words and phrases, and the attempt to ignore this fact produced gibberish too often for the system to be usable.

Furthermore, study of the contexts relevant for understanding suggest that this is itself a very complex issue. A vast collection of mutual but often implicit understandings lies behind the sharing of a common language by two people. In spoken or written discourse, reference is constantly being made to this collection of mutual understandings. But the understandings themselves are very difficult to specify, both because there are so many of them and because they are implicit. Thus, when going from one language to another by computer, it seems that one must first understand the relevant mutual understandings of both languages, then develop a set of rules that relate texts in both languages to respective mutual understandings, and finally form a theory of transformation of word-strings with attached understandings from one language to the other. Work has hardly begun on this very complex task.

As context, or the web of mutual understandings of co-linguists, becomes a relatively more important factor in language, another factor has tended to become relatively less important: syntax, or the rules of grammatical structure. This occurs inevitably; there is only 100 percent to be explained, so if context is taking an increasing share, other factors will be taking a decreasing share. The fact is that context is often a very good substitute for structure, so that though the formalities of language become devices which on occasion can be used to resolve ambiguities, they have simply lost the central place they once had in the thinking of students of language. Formal consistency or logical coherence is not a primary necessity for conveying meanings in most circumstances.

What is the nature of the web of mutual understandings that constitutes the context of communication between co-linguists? In thinking about science, we have already an answer to hand: the framework or world-view that scientists have in common, plus their common experiences—whether in the laboratory, at the blackboard, or in the library of shared readings. It is from this body that the speaker or writer feels free to draw in talking or writing to a colleague. Unless he is very fluent indeed, when he attempts to use another language for communication, his speech thins out, loses much of its punch, and tends toward the superficial and even the incomprehensible at times. Before we can ask a computer to perform even this task, some way must be found to simulate in a computer program the more important of the shared experiences of the invisible college. At any rate, it is perhaps not surprising that young Soviet economists, in studying western mathematical and statistical works on economics, picked up in their reading a good deal more than a set of value-neutral techniques. With no computer intervening, some substantial portion of the liberal's web of mutual understandings seems to have been communicated through the medium of these scientific texts.

Language and the Philosophy of Science

Kuhn's theory of science, as used in the first two parts of this book, has no explicit theory of knowledge, but his view is implicitly that science is a consensus-system.[4] We know, in the scientific sense, those things that the appropriate college of qualified experts can agree to. That is not a very satisfying epistemology; for example, it gives no clue as to why agreement is reached more easily by some invisible colleges than others. Nevertheless, it does point to the central role that communication, and hence language, plays in science. Even the positivist tradition required that knowledge be publicly testable, and this could only occur with the assistance of language.

The central importance of language, plus its complexity, pose a large number of difficult philosophical questions. Essentially the philosophical investigations of the last generation into this question have had more destructive than constructive consequences. Destructively, what has happened is that the positivist tradition has been shattered, its formulas rejected for naïveté or error or both. Constructively, perhaps one could say that it has now become clear that facts, theories, and values are inextricably intertwined in communication—scientific or otherwise. The program for further progress [5] now consists of analyzing the ways in which key terms and concepts are used in order to understand what we mean when we use them. This is a far cry from the positivist program, which separated these three elements and had a plan for developing the analysis of at least two of them that was to culminate in the construction of a "well-formed language" which would consistently embody the principles of the program. But that ambitious program did fail, and we are now back to the drawing-board stage, attempting to find ways to improve here and there our understanding of how we come to know things.

We will return to this question in connection with both verification and values. The principal point at the moment is the failure of positivism. The neat picture of the value-neutral science, of the hypothesis accepted or rejected solely on the basis of systematically accumulated and processed data, of theory as the device for testing the existing collection of hypotheses for mutual consistency and for generating new hypotheses to test—this picture cannot be sustained in the face of what is now known about the nature of language, not to mention what is known about the actual practice of scientists. The nature of its replacement is not yet well known, but it will be messier, less consistent. There is no grand Turing machine for ordinary language, which can appraise its power by means of one or two fundamental characteristics.

Another possibility has somewhat dimly emerged in recent years, which constitutes a sort of Kantian revival. In linguistics the notion is associated with the name of Chomsky and is called "deep structure." The deep structure of a language represents a collection of fundamental meanings, possibly assembled in unique forms of word-strings. Possibly the deep structure is universal, in the sense that human beings are programmed to look at the world in common ways that are captured, at least in part, by the collection of linguistic transforms embedded in the deep structure. This opens up an interesting line of speculation and perhaps suggests grounds for optimism as to whether the consensus of invisible colleges of scientists can eventually be translated to other arenas—for example, the political. But it is only a speculation at the moment.[6]

One final notion—the language game—requires a comment. Wittgenstein's term refers, in part, to the process of learning, which often includes learning ways to express novelties in language. Among the many subtle points Wittgenstein brings out in his somewhat disjointed and aphoristic discussion, is the importance of intention in communication. By varying the context and intent of the communicants, it is possible for a simple word like "slab" dramatically to change its function in the communication process. But this is not just a matter of our language using the "same" word for a variety of different purposes; this variability is built into the structure of existence, so to speak. Not only the words, but the rules for their use, change from situation to situation. This is one of the ways in which language is used to convey the uniqueness of situations even though the words themselves are not neologisms. Of course this kind of communication requires much more than passive reception of well-defined signals.

The language game was used very effectively by Wittgenstein [7] to convey the sense of the richness, singularity, and formal messiness of language. It also suggests the aliveness of language: the fact that it grows and changes with experience. But if language changes with experience, it becomes difficult, perhaps impossible, to say the old things and have them *mean* quite the old things. Language seems frequently to be regarded as a sort of ether of social science, establishing an absolute reference point by means of which standards of comparison can be constructed. But this need not be true; probably in times of change it is grossly misleading to suppose that it is true. The irreversibility suggested by the pliability of language is a major factor to be taken into account in considering the process of making at least major decisions.

Existential Man and Social Man

The existentialists are the group which has in our age come to stand for insistence on the closely interactive role of the inner man, other humans, and the environment. Most of all they have emphasized the fragmentation of the inner man in their works and the need for a sense of wholeness to one's existence as prerequisite for the realization of one's potential.

The reader who dips into existentialist literature comes away from the experience with a sense of overarching gloom and pessimism. The tone is certainly there, an emphasis on the pathology of existence, on the depths to which Angst, fragmentation, and hopelessness have driven man, whether he be a certified neurotic or not. But there is another message there, based on the prospect that a whole—an integral—existence is possible and that individuals can be converted by some process or other to the achievement of such integrity. There is a depth to the best existentialist writings that has found no reflection in the vulgarizations that have so far been about all that has made its way into the arena of political and economic discussion. Perhaps integration of the self is worth as much serious discussion in economics as integrability conditions.[8]

At any rate, the essential point for the present chapter is the interactive and social nature of the process of internal change in human development. The development of self through action, whether or not the action involves a crisis state for the individual, is a process. The essentially social nature of language makes it a basic support for the deep interdependence among human beings in their thought as well as in their behavior. Experience does not leave the individual unchanged, or if it does there is a presumption of failure of the individual or of triviality of the experience. Here again we have a view antithetical to the decision-theoretic approach.

9

Social Man and Economics

The picture of both man and language sketched in the last two chapters is clearly different from that presented in either of the two types of economic science. In this essentially methodological exercise we make no attempt to construct a clear alternative to the conventional views of economists. The aim is rather to sensitize economists to the existence of an alternative and to the need for it to be given a careful appraisal within the framework of the science. In the present chapter a few comments are offered, first on how neoclassical economics has gone astray in terms of this competing theory, second on the sorts of modifications to conventional theory the competitor may entail, and finally on the relation of the competitor to contemporary Marxism.

Language and Information

Probably it is no coincidence that information became a topic of major interest in neoclassical economics only when it appeared to offer a powerful argument against the efficiency of a socialist economy. The argument goes roughly as follows. In a competitive economy each individual agent, whether consumer or businessman, needs to know only a very limited amount of information in order to get the best possible collection of deals for himself. Specifically, he needs to know his own tastes for the various goods, or the technical capabilities of his factory if he is a businessman, and the prices of all goods. Given this information, he can maximize his own welfare. This is true for every other agent as well, so the economy has reached its best possible state, unless some change occurs in tastes or technology,[1] or unless income is redistributed among the individuals. Any other form of economic organization will either require more information or will simply be trying to simulate the competitive capitalist approach.

This looks like a good argument, until one begins to look into the assumptions on which it rests. The basic problem, which dominates a good deal of the economic analysis of information to date, is that it is static and based only on the informational requirements for sustaining an already achieved equilibrium. The individual needs only this much information because he has no ability to change prices by his own behavior and because he does not need to make predictions about future price changes. It is static also in the sense that new goods are left entirely out of account.

As soon as one places the individual in an economy where there may be imbalances between supply and demand, uncertainty regarding the future, and changes in the nature and qualities of the goods available, the information picture changes dramatically. In order to find out whether the price of a good is likely to *change* in the near future, one needs to know something about the factors that cause that price to change. There are a great many such factors in every interesting case, including not only the prices of other goods, but also the inventories presently held, the new capacity coming into production, and so on. Any decision regarding investment by a businessman is still more complicated and requires a good knowledge of the planned behavior of competitors, including those who are producing different goods that can serve as substitutes. For new goods, the problem is still more complicated and may require fancy market-studies to generate the needed information. Literally no one attempts to compare the information required under a market-system in which such difficulties arise with its socialist opposite number. In fact, there is not yet available a theory that would make such a comparison feasible.

Some economists have tried to treat information like a commodity. In that case there is no problem in integrating it into economic theory, it is simply the "n+lth good" in the list of things available for sale, and people buy information or sell it so long as it is profitable to do so. This, too, is a superficially appealing approach which is doomed to failure. Information has too many properties that are inconsistent with its being a simple commodity. For example, it is nonappropriable: I have no basis for knowing how valuable a piece of information is until I have been told what it is, but from that point on I have lost my incentive to pay for it. Consequently a market for information cannot allocate informational resources efficiently, even in principle. Furthermore, interesting information is often unique, so that aggregation, as in a market, is introduced at the cost of denying new information's most important property.[2]

This by no means exhausts the problems posed for neoclassical economics once it is recognized that information is a central ingredient in the economic process. But these difficulties with the information process, serious as they are, are not the main ones that are suggested by the preceding chapters. The two features given emphasis there are the instilling of a common language into the participants through a social process and the development of that language with experience. These features are the ones most likely to stimulate conversions.

Marxists have not attempted to introduce any such mechanical notions of information into their analyses. Marx's principle of the class domination of world-view, plus the relative reluctance to get involved with problems of detail, have saved them from such naïvetés. Indeed, the adherents of the "early Marx" orientation today are making a serious effort to get existentialist insights into their theories. Given the primarily Continental basis of twentieth-century Marxist thought, this is not surprising.

Nevertheless, it is simply not true that Marxism is equipped to apply these new notions, for as we have argued, there is much fundamental inconsistency between orthodox and early-Marx orientations, and much of it is at the philosophical level. This current Marxian crisis, in the Kuhnian sense, can probably be resolved by the crisis techniques of trying to develop an integral orientation based partly on elements of traditional Marxism. Should it precede comparable developments in revising neoclassical economics, it might change quite dramatically the relative scientific power of the two systems. At any rate, when it comes to the appreciation of the role of language in economic activity, Marxism currently has a clear conceptual edge over the neoclassicals, though again without detailed understanding; [3] what the neoclassicals do have is a lot of fancy but largely irrelevant theory.

Changing Preferences

Many economists are prepared to accept the possibility that the preferences of individual consumers change significantly. The problem is that this openmindedness cannot be translated into research in an acceptable way. The study of consumption is one of the weaker areas of performance of contemporary economics. There are very serious data problems, as always in economics, but these are compounded by conceptual problems which have come to be built into the puzzles of mainline research. It is already essentially beyond present capabilities to generate reliable measures of the demand for various goods, taking account of possible influences from the behavior of markets for substitute and complementary goods, and from goods whose demand is derived from the demand for other goods. To add to these empirical puzzles consideration of possible changes in tastes of consumers would serve, not to make the puzzles more interesting, but simply to destroy them. The very disappointing performance of neoclassical economic science in this area is one of the better arguments for casting about for a more rewarding way of dealing with the problems of the individual and family in the modern economy. However, the best argument remains, not the poor performance of the discipline in dealing with its own puzzles, but the clearly increasing irrelevance of the traditional puzzles themselves to the issues of the day.

Nevertheless, before describing the way which seems most promising to the author for dealing with this phenomenon, let us run through some of the situations in which tastes or preferences are likely to change. Many of these are quite trivial. The impulse-buying of trinkets and treats, whether in airline terminals or at the supermarket checkout line, is perhaps the most trivial—a sudden surge of desire which quickly fades. Since such buying is often of gifts or treats for others, it is also a trivial and very common instance of the interdependence of preferences. The image-building sort of advertising campaigns are a quite similar phenomenon, except that their influence on taste presumably is more durable.

A more interesting change of preferences occurs with the acceptance by consumers of a new good. Here the formal case for preference-change is unimpeachable; the arguments of any revealed preference function have changed by definition. More fundamentally, the informational requirements for acceptance make the case for a change of preferences very strong, and suggest that the integration of an attitude toward the new good will be accompanied by relative changes in attitudes toward other goods.

This latter is one way in which the interdependence of goods extends the scope of the effects of some change in preferences. If the given good has substitutes or complements, any change in tastes toward it will probably induce changes in the others. But this is not the only way in which goods are interdependent. For many decades it has been recognized that attitudes are affected by activities. As Frank Knight put it over forty years ago:

> Psychologists began a long generation ago, with the advent of the James-Lange theory, to hold that feeling results from action rather than action from feeling; that we desire because we act rather than act because we feel desire. Accepting this view, we should have to say that a consumer feels a desire for a good because he purchases it.[4]

There is no need to associate this phenomenon with such mild pathologies as classic cognitive dissonance. Learning by doing is not just a matter of improving average performance; perhaps its primary component is the change in attitudes that accompanies an improvement in skill, and in particular the desire to exercise the newly acquired skill. No one who has observed the developing consumption-patterns of such hobbyists as photographers, yachtsmen, or motorcycle racers, can doubt that a quite fundamental and broad *pattern* of changing tastes accompanies the process, even if he is not forced to endure the changes in their conversational patterns.

Changing jobs is probably a substantial inducer of taste-change, and one would expect the effect to be greater, the more substantial the job change. Among the relevant changes are those in leisure-time energy-levels; the amount of leisure time; housing, clothing, and entertainment expenditures; patterns of friendship; and the consequences of attendant effects on other members of the family. The set of job opportunities available to an individual is likely to be far less extensive and divisible than for most of the set of feasible consumption opportunities. This discontinuity is a major inducement to attitude change, especially though not entirely because of the "James-Lange" line of causation.[5]

Finally, there is the class of preference-changes which can be associated with the development of personality. This can be partly attributed to causes such as the ones just mentioned. However, the most fundamental observable of personality-changes occurs as a simple accompaniment of physiological maturation, and of the interaction of developing individuals within the family. It is probably within the capability of current neoclassical economics to devise a sort of standard, constant-income bill of goods which varies, *ceteris paribus,* merely with the physiological age of the consumer; no one could doubt that dramatic changes would occur in this market basket of goods as the standard consumer aged.

This list should suffice to indicate the vast range of situations in which changes of preferences can be expected to play an important role in consumption decisions. The typical response of the professional economist to such commentary is that the list looks fine, and the writer should be encouraged to try and pin his speculations down empirically.[6] But that is not really a serious reaction. For, as has been said before, the available empirical methodology cannot handle satisfactorily even the very restricted range of consumption-problems to which it is currently addressed. The difficulties inherent in further complicating this conventional problem seem overwhelming. The situation is rather like that of a fifteenth-century Ptolemaic astronomer faced with the need for a couple of new series of epicycles to explain planetary motions. Only by re-posing the problem can one hope to provide a basis for the development of the theory of the individual in the economy to a point at which formal empirical research can be expected to yield much fruit. The criticism that neoclassical economists should be expected to answer is that they have failed to confront this fundamental issue of economics.

Identities

The fashionable term for a persisting pattern of behavior these days is lifestyle. There is a connotation of superficiality about it, suggesting that it is a sort of clothing for the personality; more important, in usage it seems to connote that a single individual has but a single mode of behavior. For this reason alone, one might prefer a term such as "role" or "identity." We have chosen the latter because its connotations not only permit multiplicity but hint at some connection between any given identity and the deeper features of human motivation and cognition.

As one moved down the list of types of preference-changes in the last section, the idea of a pattern of behavior related to some more fundamental and coherent motivation, perhaps began to emerge. The hobbyist's identity controls one set of behaviors of the individual, while an identity associated with work or family or mistress may control others. For some individuals, all these behaviors may be quite well integrated, so that "shifting gears" as one moves from one mode of behavior to another may not occur; at the other extreme the separation may be nearly complete, and something approaching a personality transformation may accompany the change in mode of behavior. There may be a fundamental identity which to some extent dominates the others, or there may not; there is probably no such thing as a fragmented identity, but there may well be identityless individuals, and even a well-integrated person may have a variety of fragmented behaviors that do not relate in a meaningful way to any identities.

No attempts will be made to support the above assertions. Our modest aim is to suggest the way in which this approach to the individual may be applied in developing a more useful theory of worker-consumer behavior. Consequently the reader is asked to suspend judgment on the realism of the above, and to consider what one might do with the orientation, given that it is acceptable. How can it be tied fruitfully to the individual acting in the economy?

The emphasis throughout this part has been on the social nature of consumption, a view that of course has been held by numerous economists throughout the last hundred years, though it has never been a conventional topic of study in neoclassical economics. The conventional categorization of consumption and the conventional modes of aggregation discourage attempts to specify such causal connections, being tied really much more to the needs of the production sector which, in fact, is the major consumer of such demand-studies as do exist. Identities, conceived as patterns of consumption and work behavior over some limited range of both activities and goods, lend themselves much better to the analysis of social determinants.

Perhaps more important, the notion of identity lends itself better to understanding the social issues raised by the relative malleability of the individual in a modern economy. With respect to an identity, one can get a much clearer picture as to whether there is excessive product differentiation, whether the available goods can be formed by the individual into a pattern that serves the needs of the identity, whether levels and varieties of quality are adequate, and whether the means for understanding the goods-and-services component of practicing the identity are available. To test these assertions the reader is invited to try them out on himself in terms of his own vocation or avocation.

The connection between an identity and a bill of goods is of course not one-to-one. Serious photographers of some given level of skill may use a considerable variety of goods and qualities of products; they may or may not own a darkroom, may or may not work with color, etc. The great variety of such packages that can be put together in a country like the United States is a considerable tribute to the operation of the market economy (though in this case perhaps more a tribute to the Japanese production-system). Information on the activity is available through a considerable variety of media from commercial magazines to college majors. Voluntary associations of hobbyists and professionals are available in cities of any size. There are some deficiencies in this system,[7] but probably it is one of the better examples of decentralized, market-intensive support for an identity.

Another example of support for a somewhat similar identity in the American economy is that of the motorcyclist. Much the same sort of variation in level of commitment, skill, and choice of consumption patterns, occurs for the motorcyclist. However, certain features of the activity are dramatically altered in this case. Riding off the road often has harmful effects on the environment. Controls on off-road riding not infrequently produce the tragic phenomenon of a young man with a new trail bike and no place to ride it. Still worse is the situation of the road rider, who tends to be young and unaware of the risks he runs, especially in the first few weeks of practicing his hobby. The peculiar psychological attractions of the motorcycle can lead to a stunted identity-structure and to very risky styles of riding, among the less important of which are the "identity" pressures against the wearing of helmets. Finally, racing is a highly commercialized and vulgarized activity to which considerable risks are attached and in which large numbers of young men, often still in their teens, participate under the overwhelming pressures of ego-gratifying fathers. Clearly, there are many things wrong with this primarily market-supported identity.

These two characterizations of identities are quite casual and should not be taken too seriously (I suspect that more careful study would show up a few more problems in photography, and probably in motorcycling, too). Again, they are designed to suggest the way in which the notion of an identity provides guidelines for the analysis of consumption. In particular, they offer a basis for dealing in an integral way with both externalities and market phenomena. Furthermore, the identity seems to be more closely tied to our understanding of humans than is the notion of *homo economicus* with his insatiability, declining marginal utilities, and rational choice over some infinite commodity space.

Three concepts that play virtually no role in the conventional theory of consumption, but that are of central importance for anyone concerned with real-world issues relating to consumption, are anxiety, alienation, and solidarity. Each of these concepts lends itself at least partly to incorporation into an identity-analysis of consumption. Anxiety may be associated with the fear of losing an identity—with the probability that the activities associated with the identity are going to lose their satisfying quality. Alienation may be associated with a special form of ignorance—with the absence of an identity which can give one guidance as to satisfying future behavior. And solidarity may be associated with the sharing of an identity or role, its values and commitments and skills. These associations by no means exhaust the content of the three concepts. But they do suggest ways in which identities can be used to integrate at least a portion of their significance into economics, and ways in which lines of empirical research could be opened up.

A threefold classification of identities might have them either integral, flawed, or false. The notions are self-explanatory, but it seems that the above concepts may be used to help make such a classification. For example, if the phenomenon of solidarity is observed as a strong and ubiquitous accompaniment of certain identities, this would probably be taken as evidence that the identity was integral: capable of providing fundamental satisfactions to the individual. Anxiety associated with an identity, suggests that it is flawed or ephemeral, or at any rate that it is no longer integral for the respective individuals. And alienation is a sign that the assumed identities have not become integral for the relevant individuals. Interesting design implications for the social system might very well flow from such analyses, and that is rather more than one can say for the current theory.

Not all preference changes can reasonably be assigned to changes in identities. Some—impulse buying, for example—are too ephemeral for that, or are too trivial to be accessible to such analysis. The improvement of a flawed identity may be difficult to distinguish, in terms of purchasing habits, from identity change, and so forth. But the idea that consumption and work behavior is tied to a set of patterns whose interdependence is captured by the concept of an identity does seem to reflect a substantial reality. At least as important is the prospect of tying these changes to their social (and perhaps physiological-developmental) determinants, a feat that economists have not begun to attempt.

The Great Surplus Game, Or Adding N-Ach to Galbraith

It is no easy matter to get a reasonably talented young man really excited about selling soap. But corporations have found a way to do this. It is not just a matter of rewarding performance handsomely, and is not principally a matter of offering security. It is much more like joining an exclusive club in which rather strict rules of comportment are laid down, and where all members participate in a competitive game. The initiation fee for joining the club consists in making a commitment to the success of the club, with the attendant implications for playing the game, the commitment being verified during an apprenticeship or probation period. Clubhouse activities are quite important, for this is one of the best ways for older members to check up on the genuineness of the younger members' commitment, including of course their respect for authority and for the successful.

Nevertheless, the heart of the corporate system lies in the game itself. Here we are most concerned with the players, their motivations, and the system's responsiveness. In recruitment and early training, men with a high need for achievement, in McClelland's sense,[8] are sought. They are ambitious, but they also have a particular attitude toward risk and skill. Long shots are avoided in career building because they constitute an essentially random process, so that the winners are undistinguished from the losers by any factor other than their luck. Sure things are uninteresting because again success is not a measure of the man. What the participants want, or are taught to want, are situations of medium risk, where the odds can be altered by the skill of the player. Such people become restless when faced with nothing but sure things and uneasy when the odds grow too long.

Risk seems to play a double role. In the first place it is a stimulus, adding spice to the game. But it is also a cover for failure: it is possible for the winner to credit his skill for the victory, the loser to blame his luck for the defeat, and for the other players to react in ways that promote the solidarity of the club or their own egos. Finally, the manipulability of the risk is an important part of the skill of the game.

The corporate game is organized so as to reward this type of player. Corporate hierarchies are pyramided so as to provide a reasonable chance for promotion for participants at most stages. The executive market serves to stabilize these risks, so that executives in a too sharply pyramided corporation are not constrained to an excessively risky environment. Tasks are divided and decentralized so that individuals and small teams can be identified with the success or failure of each significant operation, and much effort is devoted to providing rules that establish, within achievement-oriented risk levels, measures of performance. Within this framework the ambitious (and hitherto successful) executive thrives on risk rather than avoiding it. But nothing makes him so anxious as situations, such as the aerospace industry has been experiencing, in which the risks have become long and largely escape his control.

Within this context, forms of competition that satisfy the needs of the game are not merely tolerated but actively sought. The game cannot be played without opponents, and the opponents must also observe the rules so as to permit assessment of risks and to stabilize them. The theory of oligopolistic competition has concentrated on a profit-maximizing criterion for performance, which hardly fits the facts of corporate structure, is unable to select among alternative attitudes toward risk, and consequently is nearly empty of content. Viewing this sort of competition as a social (not game-theoretic) game with rules which have been structured by the established identities of the players, may offer a real prospect for generating some results. For example, it is easy to imagine situations in which price competition *would* occur in this environment. One of the most likely is the shaking out of a new-product market, which is done by rather intense price competition led by powerful corporations who are in effect attempting to establish a market environment that will permit institutionalization of the game. Risk of corporate ruin is not within the game's acceptable risk levels. By eliminating the small fry in this case, the corporate system is adapting competition to fit their rules, especially since their major competitors are all members of the club with credentials established in other industries.

Viewed in this light, diversification and the conglomerate movement appear partly as attempts to establish an environment within which a sufficient set of achievement games can be developed. Risk of ruin for the corporation must be kept very low, for it is clearly not an achievement risk, being too fraught with unevaluable uncertainties even for the top leadership of the corporation. But new product development within a context of overall stability is one of the most promising of games: even products as expensive as Edsels fit within this framework of acceptable risk for the major participants. Stockholders are of course not members of the club, but they do serve to define some of the more important rules of the game, and the participants are indeed constrained by them.

A good deal more could be said in this vein, but our present purpose is quite limited. Clearly this interpretation of corporate behavior puts identity in a central place in the interpretation and raises social issues related to corporate behavior in a rather different context than is customary. The formal object of the activity, providing certain goods and services to the consumer, assumes a purely symbolic function in this interpretation. Soap or automobiles or pharmaceuticals need have no more intrinsic importance for the players than a baseball does for another group of social gamesmen. It is therefore not surprising that even quite goodhearted performers are hardly aware of the social significance of their activity and do not respond very coherently to criticism. Furthermore, outside intervention to change the rules tends to be vigorously fought on grounds that seem quite moral to the participants; the insensitive outsider does not understand the sensitivity of the game itself to rule changes and may destroy the game for the players without realizing it. Nevertheless, the social need for outside control of the game is quite clear, given the symbolic—for the players—nature of what economists call performance.

The identity question poses dilemmas of control both inside and outside the game. Players often express their concern over "sharks": participants who have acquired enough power to influence the environment of others but who violate the rules, either by taking unusual risks or by violating some of the behavioral rules that are designed to control general systemic risks (mergers as viewed by executives in the smaller firms are an example). Then, too, there is the problem of the losers, of those who have lost their expectation of making it to the next stage, of winning the next round of their game. Such people are no longer able to play the game, but to eliminate them ruthlessly is probably inconsistent with achievement-level risks for the continuing players. These and other problems of failures of the hypothetically desired incentive-system pose continuing problems for those who are engaged in preserving the game. That identity crises often accompany severance from the main line of play suggests that in fact indoctrination into the rules of the game is a fundamental feature.

Social control of corporate behavior should take account of whether we have a more effective alternative to the current structuring of identities. That social responsibility might actually be instilled is certainly a possibility, but it could hardly work without simultaneous change in the rules of the game. Nationalization is not much of an answer if it does not take account of the identities a civil service structure instills, and the behaviors that are likely to result. Even nationalized soap may not sing for the participants, so maybe some more suitable game will have to be devised.

Social games may decline and fall as a result of internal processes, but most survival issues are likely to involve change from outside the social system of the game. One possibility is that in a given environment the game becomes self-destructive after a time. For example, ventures with the appropriate risk-structure could be destroyed if the merger movement continued to the point of substantial monopoly. The surplus game seems very closely tied to growth: if growth should slow substantially, that basic element of the game, the venture with appropriately structured risks, could become too scarce to support the game's structure. Another possibility is that social change outside the corporate structure would begin to inhibit the process of identity establishment and maintenance. A rise of anxiety and the sense of alienation among participants would signal such a change on this interpretation, for these are major signs of a fading or lost identity. The social destructiveness of the game could of course lead to intervention; among its more important destructive effects may well be the stunting of the extragame lives of executives because of the very great demands of the game. But of course the most important risk to society at large of such a game is the social irresponsibility that is indirectly instilled through the process of establishing identities.

The name "surplus game" seems appropriate because in most Marxian definitions most of the resources that go into this game come out of that part of the social pie; indeed, on the fate-control interpretation of exploitation, this is *all* surplus. From a Marxist point of view the surplus game would be an elaborate and probably unselfconscious device for channeling energies into the process of allocating the surplus under conditions of increasing waste. Viewed that way, it has been one of the great successes of the capitalist system. Evidence abounds that a great many of the players really enjoy the game and identify with it, and it seems currently to be in the process of conquering Europe. Nevertheless, it has serious krakh-potential. The requisite identity may be fragile with respect to contemporary lifestyle challenges, and to increasing understanding of the consequences of the game. Also, the environment seems to be demanding increasing public control of business activity, which can seriously threaten its risk structures. At any rate, if this game exists it would seem to be worth careful study.

Conclusion

Conversions can be usefully analyzed by means of identities. The range of economic activities for which conversions play an important role is at least that of the economy itself. Contemporary consumption theory is virtually useless for the major issues of policy that have to be faced today.

Little account has been taken of Marxism in this part. The reason is that in this area of thought Marxists have largely suffered from the same type of orientation as the clinical psychologist. Their primary interest has been in the pathology of behavior, and even by indirection they do not have a plausible theory of the "whole" man. For orthodox Marxists, who put deterministic emphasis on the impersonal causal line from mode of production (technology) to the nature of man, this is perhaps acceptable. But for the early Marxists it is not; the issues raised by generation, adoption, and rejection of identities by both society and individuals must be faced directly by them and a theory which relates social instruments to psychological satisfactions developed. That has yet to be done.

Part IV

The Art of Persuasion

10

oooooooooooooooooooooooooooooooooooooooooooooooooooooooooooooooooo

Verification in Economics

Input

The formalist revolution in postwar economics was solidly based on the methodological dream of the latter day positivists. The translation of economic problems into a formal, rather mathematical language, was designed to fulfill one of the primary positivist aims: the construction of a well-formed language, of great precision, in which a clear distinction between meaningful and other types of statements could be made. The threefold separation of fact, value, and theory was carefully preserved. This new language of economics was one in which not much discussion of alternative values would take place. Values were separated out to appear in isolated criteria, whose value the various agents under study were presumed to maximize, and whose arguments were such positive, observable variables as outputs, inputs, and prices. Theory was separated from fact. The central element of theory was the model, the device by which various assumptions could be logically combined and manipulated to generate hypotheses. These latter provided the point of contact with fact. Facts consisted of pools of data, essentially numbers purporting to describe some aspect of economic behavior, numbers which could be regarded as groupable in such a way that all members of a group constituted observations of the same theoretical phenomenon. Statistical techniques then provided the means for testing whether or not the appropriate group of observations was consistent with the appropriate hypothesis.

The aim of the formalist revolution was to transform all economics into this framework. As seen from the vantage point of twenty years ago, this seemed to many of the best, and particularly to most of the best young, minds in economics to be a noble aim. If successful, it offered great advantages over the older verbal and intuitive and "statistics-without-theory" schools of thought. The achievement could be expected to provide a substantial integration of all of economics. Because theorists were using a common language, the connections among theories could be easily seen and common groundworks laid. In the new language the theories themselves would be cast in terms that invited, rather than discouraged, empirical testing. The link through statistics meant that interactive growth of theory and applied work would be assured. And the statistical theory itself assumed a novel and central place. By developing techniques for appraising hypotheses the investigator would be provided with a hard basis for knowing just how much he did *not* know. Given the exalted claims that were often made for ideas which had no clearcut links with the real world, even this somewhat negative property appeared as fundamental progress. If all this could be done —and by 1950 a good start had been made all around, though the practitioners were still few—economics could take its place as a fullfledged science in the strictest positivist sense of the word.

Not only was this a noble aim, but it appeared to be attainable. The old mathematical-economics tool of the calculus had been sharpened by Samuelson and others, who injected more sophisticated mathematics into the study of traditional microeconomics. Perhaps even more promising, a "new math" based on modern algebra, of which linear programming and activity-analysis were the major tools, opened up the possibility of directly applying this traditional theory in practical problems. Even more exciting was the fact that these new techniques seemed essentially to vindicate the older theory, to provide empirical support for the traditional economic analysis of the price system. The Keynesian revolution provided a theoretical base to which mathematics was readily applicable, and in which the mathematics was proving itself in just the expected way: the precision of expression that the mathematics required was a major factor in resolving some of the ambiguities of formulation of which verbal theorists, including Keynes, had been guilty. The development of national income accounting, especially in the United States, was beginning to offer a pool of data that was consciously adapted to some of the needs of the macroeconomist. Statistical techniques were being developed that already made the hypothesis-testing operation a far more sophisticated and powerful operation than it had been only a decade or so earlier. In effect, economics was already tooled up for the major effort of reconstruction—an effort that was intellectually challenging even to first-rate minds and that held out as great a promise for the welfare of mankind as perhaps any scholarly activity of the time.

Output

Well, of course, the effort was made. Every major economics department in the United States that trains significant numbers of Ph.D.'s has dramatically altered its personnel in accordance with the requirements of the formalist approach. Hundreds of man-years of the best talent available to the discipline have been directed to bringing the positivist dream to reality in economics. From our new vantage point twenty years later, we can now ask, What are its fruits? Unfortunately we can make no serious attempt at appraisal. This would be an extraordinarily difficult task, and probably pointless, for reasons that will emerge. All that is attempted in the next couple of pages is to outline the kind of case that can be made for the substantial failure of the revolution.

1 The tremendous quality and quantity of the inputs that have been put into the formalist revolution have certainly generated a largescale output in the form of models, hypotheses, and tests. All the techniques described above, and a number of others besides, have been widely applied. The advice of economists is sought very widely in both business and government. And increasingly, right up to the present, the economists sought are those capable of working within the formalist framework. In addition, as mentioned earlier, these same techniques have begun to be applied to problems that lie in fields adjacent to economics. All this is very positive with respect to the positivist approach.

2 However, a closer look at any of the main areas of research is a bit troubling. Take the forecasting of the performance of the economy in the shortrun, for example. This is the area of Keynesian economic policy *par excellence* and so has tended to attract a relatively large fraction of economists who have a strong policy orientation. But what one finds here is that the forecasts are not working too well. In fact, these big models, in which as much as a million dollars of research funds may be invested, have been performing so poorly in recent months that some of those with the best reputations are reputedly inserting "fudge-factors" to get a better prediction of price-changes than the models can give. That is, the economists have the laborious calculations entailed in using the model to forecast carried out on the computer, and then jack up the price data that comes out by a few points, because they have more faith in their own intuitive judgment than in these great empirically estimated models.

One of the standard tests of performance of models such as these is to compare the quality of their predictions with those of rather mechanistic "naïve models." An example of the latter would be simply to predict that, say, the 1971–1972 change in output and employment will be the same as that which occurred in 1970–1971. It takes no big research grant to finance a naïve model, and virtually no theory either, so it is a very weak test of a sophisticated model's performance. Time after time these naïve tests perform about as well as the models against which they are tested; not infrequently they perform better. This applies not just to Keynesian models of the economy—and not just to models of the United States—but to many other techniques as well, such as the input-output analysis that is so widely applied in socialist and developing countries as well as the United States and Western Europe.

3 Another troubling feature of empirically estimated models is their unsatisfactory econometric status. Most of the models violate fundamental canons of hypothesis testing—for example, by testing a variety of forms for a particular equation, selecting the one that fits the data best, and then adjusting the theoretical model so that it constitutes a defense of the hypothesis that was actually chosen from analysis of the same data used to "test" the hypothesis. A second breach of econometric faith is a sort of hidden fudge-factor. The practitioner adjusts parameters that have previously been estimated statistically on the basis of *a priori* information (which may be no more than a hunch), and then puts the adjusted model to work. The user may be completely unaware of this, and is unlikely to be given any hint as to its formal effect on the inference-properties of the model. In these and a number of other ways the independence of hypothesis and data, a fundamental part of the positivist dream, is ubiquitously violated.

But in a sense these adjustments are not so significant after all, or rather they pale somewhat before the more fundamental fact that nobody really believes that any formal information has been generated about the inference-properties of the model: that is, about the extent to which it gives, formally speaking, a good causal picture of reality. The problem here is the amount of data available. Even if no forbidden adjustments were made and the assumptions about the model and data were basically true, these models are based on such small samples of data that, given their complexity, one is not formally entitled to say much of anything about what can be inferred from them.

4 Data is never wholly satisfactory. Even in the hardest parts of physics one must contend with instrument and observer error. But the sad truth about economics is that the data is not only rather thin in quantity, it is even worse in terms of quality. As one example, the rules for collection of data used by statistical agencies are changed from time to time in most time-series data, and so the earlier data can only be made comparable to the new and presumably improved series by making *post factum* adjustments. Many other problems develop in handling data, but let us pass over these to emphasize the most important point: the data rarely represent very closely the concepts which are manipulated by the theory. The neat technologies and smooth transitions and uniform behaviors that form essential ingredients of even sophisticated theory cannot be observed. Mixed into our observable surrogates is quite a lot of theory, of interpolation and assumption that even if accepted does not bring the yearbook variable to coincide with the theory's variable. I suspect that any known variable could be used as an example in support of this assertion. One might mention GNP, with its government contribution measured by the inputs (wages) of government servants rather than by their output, with consumption in kind and various other "nonmarket" variables estimated in terms of their alleged market value, and with (the most impertinent presumption of all) the tacit acceptance of the idea that upward is good regardless of the effects on income distribution.[1]

This problem of quality and representativeness is very

serious from the point of view of the positivist dream. The hypothesis-testing relies on the assumption that each observation in the sample of data is as good, as representative as every other. Standardization is the key to success in getting the ingredients for successful hypothesis-testing, positivist-style. And that is why Procrustes was the first econometrician.

5 The optimization models have their own special problems, in addition to those mentioned above in connection with data. It has always turned out to be difficult to specify a good criterion to maximize for these problems. One recalls the comments of early management scientists, that businessmen were constantly asking them what they ought to want to do. But we are not concerned with that just now. More important here has been the problem of the rigidity of the constraints in these problems. For example, one might want to find the maximum output in an industry subject to the constraint of fixed (in the short run) plant capacity, labor force, and so forth. But in practice the constraints businessmen are up against are not so sharp as this. To put it more generally, no satisfactory way has been found to characterize mathematically the environment of choice of the economic agent.

The upshot of this has been that, by and large, no one believes these models either. This is not to say that no use is made of them. But perhaps the typical reaction is: "Well, the great thing was that formally posing the problem compelled the researcher to collect his data and look at it in a systematic and thorough way." Lacunae were easy to spot because the researcher was constrained to find some way to close the problem so as to generate enough intellectual and data inputs that a formal solution would be forthcoming. This helped a lot, but the formalities essentially played the role of a sort of cookbook set of instructions as to what ingredients to assemble. The results (the "solution") were then used as inputs to the informed judgment of practitioners, not as serious descriptions of what the practitioner (businessman) ought to do.

One could continue in this vein at some length, but perhaps the point has been taken, if not accepted, by the reader. It could not be better phrased than by one of the best practitioners of formalist economics in his Presidential Address to the American Economic Association:

> . . . an uneasy feeling about the present state of our discipline has been growing in some of us who have watched its unprecedented development over the last three decades. This concern seems to be shared even by those who are themselves contributing successfully to the present boom. They play the game with professional skill but have serious doubts about its rules. . . . The uneasiness of which I spoke before is caused not by the *irrelevance* of the practical problems to which present day economists address their efforts, but rather by the palpable *inadequacy* of the scientific means with which they try to solve them. . . . the consistently indifferent performance in practical applications is in fact a symptom of a fundamental imbalance in the present state of our discipline. The weak and all too slowly growing empirical foundation clearly cannot support the proliferating superstructure of pure, or should I say, speculative economic theory.[2]

Neoclassical economics has come a long way in the last twenty years, and much that the formalists have done must be appraised positively. But it is nevertheless true that the output from all this input has been most disappointing. In the following pages various arguments are tried out in aid of the proposition that it will take more than more data to rescue the positivist dream. Basically the discussion concerns the relationship between the inputs and outputs we have just been discussing.

A Parable

"Once there were two warring tribes. They had a common nonwestern culture and a common language. Indeed, the only noticeable difference between them was in their height: one tribe's members were, on the average, six centims taller than the other's. One day early in the war a Watu patrol came upon some fifty soldiers and captured them. The captives claimed that they were Watu from an outlying village, now cut off from the main territory, but the Watu chief suspected that they might be a patrol of the hated Butusi. Some captives were taller than many Watu, and some were smaller. Interrogation was unrevealing, and while the elders were deliberating on a course of action, a tribal member who had been educated abroad suggested that a western statistician could solve their problem for them. One was immediately brought in as a consultant. He had members of the tribe provide him with relevant data: the mean heights of the two tribes and their variation, the heights of the captives, and the firm belief that no other known trait had a nonzero correlation with tribal membership. He questioned the elders about their values, and was told that they had two variables to contend with: 1) a genuine desire for justice, i.e. to avoid killing the innocent; and 2) a genuine belief that if the captives were really Butusi and were not killed they would surely escape and might affect the course of the war. After obtaining from the elders the strengths of these conflicting values and putting this data with the other relevant facts, the statistician produced a black box, cranked his information into it, and sat back. After a few moments the black box emitted a piece of paper, which the statistician read. He then rose, and turning to the Watu chief, said, 'Kill them!' (Actually, when on consultant's salary, the statistician, as a matter of principle, uttered only sentences in the indicative mood. What he really said was, 'Provided the facts you gave me are correct, and the criteria you provided me represent your true beliefs and their intensities, then if you follow your beliefs you will decide to kill the captives.') Upon returning to his western homeland the statistician wrote up his activities among the Watu in a paper which was widely regarded as a classic of positive science and of the application of statistical method to the problem of verification."

Comments

1 Judge Bridlegoose, a character from Rabelais, used to decide his cases by throwing appropriately loaded dice. As Ernest Nagel has suggested,[3] the Judge's behavior stands for the ideal of a calculus of evidence, which could be used in a wholly impersonal way to determine guilt or innocence, truth or falsehood. Well, it seems that we now have those dice, in the form of our statistician's black box. Within it are the mysterious gears that run the mechanism of statistical decision theory. We are not concerned with the engineering aspects of its design, which are the central concern of econometricians. But it is the case that the kind of information supplied by the consultant gives, with one or two adjustments, the information necessary for the black box to compute the preferred outcome, using whatever of the contemporary statistical techniques may be appropriate. The problem our consultant faces is relatively simple and clearcut, so we can safely ignore problems of choice of estimating-technique, which give much trouble in more complex problems. Essentially we are assuming away most of the problems that were listed earlier in the chapter.

2 Even so, a major choice remains for the consultant. On the side of the black box there is a dial, which is labeled "Hurwicz Optimism-Pessimism Index." [4] This must be set by the consultant and is independent of the information so far gathered. For example, let us suppose that of the four possible outcomes the tribal council believed the best possible one to be that the captives are Watu and it is decided to spare them, and the worst outcome to be that they are the hated Butusi and are spared. If our consulting statistician happens to have a rather gloomy and pessimistic attitude toward nature's benevolence, he will select a low or pessimistic point on the dial, which implies killing the captives. By deciding for killing, one makes certain that the worst alternative of the tribal chiefs (spared Butusi) is avoided. If he thinks nature is always playing dirty tricks on humans, he has thus prevented her from doing at least the worst possible thing. If the statistician has just the opposite attitude toward nature, his choice of a high point on the Hurwicz index will lead to the black box selecting the alternative "Spare them!" for only by this decision can the best possible alternative (spared Watu) be feasible. Note that the available information provided by the council about their beliefs is being used in the black box; for example, it provided the ranking of alternatives (and the intensity of those beliefs as well). But even so, the decision depends importantly, even vitally, on the world-view of the consultant.[5]

3 The parable poses in a rather extreme form some of the dilemmas of professionalism. The esoteric knowledge of the professional gives him a great deal of power. It is no accident, and no evidence of chicanery, that politicians prefer to get their expert advice from experts who share their own political orientation. The politician is merely trying to ensure that this power will be working for him, not against him. But in order to do this the politician must have *some* comprehension of the nature of the expert's knowledge. Neither our council of elders nor even, in all probability, the young man educated abroad, appreciated the significance of the consultant's attitude toward nature for their solution.

4 Another dilemma of professionalism is posed by the distancing between patron and client which is built into the relationship. The consultant is not really engaged by his profession in the great drama and potential tragedy of his patrons' situation. When he gets home he is respected and arouses professional interest because he had the good fortune to deal with a problem which could be handled in a clearcut way by his techniques, and did so successfully. Much of the human situation will go unreported, and probably the human interest that appears in his accounts will be in the form of humorous asides about the difficulty of extracting relevant information from the unstatistical masses. The distancing is an inevitable, and of course quite human, response to professional specialization in dealing with social problems. To the extent that there is a standardized professional identity, there is the risk that progress within the discipline is bought at the price of rigidity and indifference to many relevant factors by the standardized practitioners.

5 The mystery of the black box must intrigue the natives enormously. But in a less dramatic way the mystery of the natives is just as fundamental for the consultant. Locked in the language of his profession, his culture, the consultant cannot obtain "unbiased" Information from his informants. The communication error resulting from this mutual mysteriousness can also be dramatic; one only has to think of the attempt to extract the ingredients for a criterion (say a quadratic loss function?) from the council; or perhaps of the attempt to translate with full accuracy the indicative-mood recommendation into the council's language.

6 Beyond the more direct consequences of distancing and impersonality, of esoteric language and knowledge-is-power, lies a much less subtle form of distortion of the solution process: the unconscious motivations and tendencies in the behaviors of all concerned, but particularly (for our purposes) of the consultant. Maybe in fact our consultant did not give serious attention to the information given him by the Watu. He merely remembered a study done by one of his students back home which showed that the value of a nonbirth in underdeveloped countries was $3,641, and figured that even with a discount for rearing the marginal social product of a Watu or a Butusi warrior was negative. Perhaps this was not a conscious process with the consultant, but was accomplished by giving the Hurwicz dial an extra twist in the pessimism direction, or perhaps biases in his understanding of fact were the device by which this factor was put into the decision process. Given the communication problems, the social tests available to other participants against this sort of manipulation are largely absent; in no situation involving communication barriers are they fully present.

7 Professional competition is the principal device by which many of these distortions are supposed to be controlled. It is undeniably effective in pushing participants toward efficient choice-procedures. The quality of the statistician's black box is subject to the control of the statistical profession; but the world-view and communications gap remain and are perhaps the most pervasive causes of the distortions we have been discussing. As has been argued above, world-view indoctrination is central to professional training, becomes part of the shared beliefs of professionals, and so lies largely outside the discipline's competitive, puzzle-solving processes.

8 Our consultant viewed his problem quite narrowly; he simply did the precise job for which he was hired. Had he viewed the problem in an open-ended way the outcome might have been different. A rented helicopter, after all, could have settled the captives' claim in a few minutes. Or failing that, escape-proof-jail-making skills might have been obtained from whichever agency was appropriate—the CIA or the Soviet Embassy. But unfortunately these are unprofessional solutions, and though the consultant might still collect his fee, there would be no paper in a learned journal when he arrived home. The professional incentive system and training program to which he has been subjected conspire to discourage the consultant from looking at the problem in this way. Competition within the profession reinforces this narrow outlook on problems.

There is some—too much—truth in the assertion that

modern econometrics is essentially a myth-building operation, an attempt to give a hard surface to a soft reality. But in a way the more serious problem may be almost the opposite of this. For the modern world has a strong tendency to adapt itself to the needs of expertise. The techniques will work better if the participants will only be willing to make rational, deliberative choices with criteria whose arguments are limited in number and easily quantifiable. A discipline that only takes "seriously" (considers professionally interesting) problems that can be fitted into this framework, and whose members have considerable impact on a broad range of policies, cannot but push society itself in this direction. The potential result, a self-justifying success which is actually a failure, is a phenomenon familiar to readers of Marcuse but is not a part of the neoclassical paradigm.

11

The Positivist Dream

Induction

The problem of induction is one of the few philosophical questions that has rather persistently engaged the attention of economists. The problem is that of justifying the leap from the particular to the general—for example, from the observation that changes in consumption and income have been associated on occasion in the past, to the assertion that they will continue to be associated. Mill, Jevons, Keynes, and Harrod, among others, put major effort into their quite different attempts to justify the inductive leap, so interest in the problem runs right down to our own day.[1] However, none of these economists' solutions are accepted today by practicing economists—Keynes's Treatise on Probability is unread and Harrod's Problem of Induction is unknown—for we take our guidance in these matters now from statisticians and positivists. Some econometricians feel obliged at least to mention the problem of induction, and such appropriate names as Savage, Jeffreys, and Popper are included in these introductory remarks.[2]

The peculiar thing about the problem of induction is that everybody already believes it, but nobody has a satisfying account of why we *should* believe it. Perhaps the philosopher Max Black has put the situation correctly:

> It is not so much that we do not know how to justify induction as that we do not know and cannot imagine what we would *accept* as such a justification. Clarity here . . . ought to result in the disappearance of . . . the problem . . . [which] will eventually be classified with such famous "insoluble" problems as that of squaring the circle . . .[3]

Unfortunately we cannot leave it there, for many economists seem to have accepted a quite mechanical "solution" to the problem, one which they use to justify application of rather mechanical verification procedures to the discipline. So a brief look will be taken at Popper's falsifiability criterion and the notion of prior probabilities, in order to put induction and verification into a more reasonable perspective.

"Conceivable falsification" is a term that pops up time and again in positivist discussions. Popper's version has been simply described by Braithwaite: "The empirical criterion of rejection for a scientific hypothesis is so fundamental that it is most convenient to treat the *meaning* of universal sentences expressing empirical generalizations as being determined by the experiences which would refute them." [4] The heart of the idea is the asymmetry between rejection and acceptance of a hypothesis. The assertion is that rejection is the more important because if a hypothesis has any empirical significance one can always think of evidence which would lead one decisively to reject the hypothesis. As for acceptance, about all one can do by empirical testing is find that the evidence does not decisively refute the hypothesis: data is essentially either "against" or "not against" the hypothesis. The picture of verification in science that emerges is one of a group of not-yet-refuted hypotheses sitting on the scientific table, with the scientists busy in their labs trying their best to refute them.

Proposed solutions to the problem of induction can be divided into two groups: those that attempt to justify induction by deduction and those that attempt to justify it by induction. Popper's approach as described above is an example of the former: conceivable falsifiability is a deductive quality since a hypothesis possesses it if one can deduce qualities, defined in terms of empirical (in principle) facts which contradict it. An example of the latter is the defense of induction on grounds that it has worked in the past. Defense of induction by induction is circular; induction by deduction smacks of the synthetic *a priori,* of generating empirical facts with pure logic, a process rigidly excluded by positivism. It is in this sense that all justifications of induction are unsatisfying.

But Popper himself did not stop his discussion of induction with his account of the falsification criterion of meaning. He realized that scientists do make inductive discriminations among the collection of "not yet disproved" hypotheses. To handle this he developed the notion of the extent of corroboration of hypotheses, which depends on the severity of the attempts to falsify them. By this route Popper (and other positivists such as Carnap) come back to an essentially probabilistic theory of induction.[5] But these theories make no real attempt to justify induction. They merely put forward some propositions that provide general guidelines for procedure in inductive inference, but that are not justified, in the sense that no attempt is made to show that the inductive leap is itself derived from inherently plausible statements. What it all boils down to is that, philosophically speaking, induction is a convention. The elegant modern structure of statistical inference and decision theory is built on a philosophical house of sand.

The starting point for these probability theories, which underly the econometric work mentioned in the last chapter, is initial or *a priori* information available to the scientist in the form of probabilities. There are various versions of the theory, but what it amounts to is that the investigator can convert what is already known about the problem into a set of probabilities about the occurrence of certain phenomena. The statistical theory then provides him with a means of combining this *a priori* information with his new information (observations) to generate his conclusion, which might, for example, be a revision of the prior probabilities with which he started. Through this process of mutual adjustment of hypotheses and observations, the pool of not yet refuted hypotheses is revised, but also probabilistic expectations are formed as to the relative survival-values of the various hypotheses in the pool.

Our verbal description of course does not do justice to the power and flexibility of the theory. One should note that one of its most striking outputs is precisely the relative degree of corroboration of hypotheses. Statisticians have tended to like the falsifiability criterion, perhaps because they have usually not been professionally concerned with the substance of the theories from which hypotheses are derived, and falsifiability provides them with the opportunity to avoid exploration of the relevance of these theories. But as economic problems and economists have come more to the fore in the development of statistical inference, this attitude has changed, and the central role that theory plays in corroboration has come to be recognized. Nowadays the investigator is expected to provide a theoretical model that "rationalizes" the hypothesis he is testing: that derives the hypothesis from some assumptions which he can defend as being more or less scientifically sound. In principle it is even possible to capture this notion of "more or less realistic" in the inference process by setting up a mathematical formula that measures the costs to the investigator of various kinds of errors in the inference. This provides an apparently very close and profound connection between the two central scientific processes of deduction and induction: deduction is used to develop a model of the relevant environment of the problem, from which the hypothesis is derived, and to develop a model of the way to perform the inductive inference. Then data is collected and processed in accord with the inductive canons. The result is a "hard" product which measures precisely what is known and even what is not known. It looks so good that perhaps one can forget the philosophy? Let us look briefly at one or two unsettled problems.

Colligation

A dozen years ago three important books on the philosophy of science appeared which possessed a common provenance and theme: Michael Polanyi's *Personal*

Knowledge, N. R. Hanson's *Patterns of Discovery,* and Kuhn's *Structure of Scientific Revolutions.*[6] All were strongly influenced by the Cambridge philosophical current flowing from Wittgenstein's renunciation of his positivist position. For each of them a central element in scientific procedure lay outside the realms of deduction and induction. Like almost everything in philosophy, this element is as old as the Greeks, and was perhaps best named a century or so ago by Whewell,[7] who called it "colligation" (literally, "tying together"—it has also been called abduction).

Essentially, colligation is the process of idea-formation. This is strictly neither inductive nor deductive, though both processes may play a role. For example, an economist may stumble upon a pool of data that has not been used before and may cast about for a way to put it to use in understanding the economy. From the existing literature, he may glean some hypotheses for which the data is relevant. More likely he will come across a segment of theory that looks relevant, and will try to derive an interesting hypothesis from it. He may even be moved to generate a new theory which "makes" the data relevant for some hypothesis. Whatever the procedure, it involves intuition engaged in the process of making some thesis or data relevant: that is, of tying the thesis to things that are already known. There are no fixed rules for colligation, but all interesting scientific work contains at least a bit of it.

The three works alluded to above have a common attitude toward colligation. They believe that it is a central part of scientific procedure and that it is closely tied to a set of implicit beliefs which members of a particular invisible college of science have in common. As Hanson put it, there is a pattern in discovery that is generated by the investigator's way of looking at the data, which in turn is generated by aspects of his background and training. To generate a "new look" at the data, something must occur to bring into question the common pattern, to generate a search for a new pattern. And as Polanyi has it, much of this background is possessed by the investigator in an inarticulate way, so that it influences his behavior, may be transmitted connotatively to students, but cannot be stated explicitly. Of course that is not true of all of the belief-system of the scientists; much of it is quite explicit and simply consists of those parts of the formal discipline which he understands.

If the story stopped here, it would not be threatening to the positivist theory of verification. For we now merely have three, instead of two, quite distinct boxes within which the various parts of scientific activity can be neatly placed. Colligation is perhaps not so well understood as the others, though improvement here can be expected by tackling those belief-systems explicitly, but perhaps that is just as well, for we don't want to take all the fun out of science by routinizing creativity anyway.

But the story will not tell that way. The closer one looks at colligative activity, the more fundamental its impact on the other ingredients becomes, and the less distinct the verbal boxes that were supposed to distinguish them. Let us consider in particular the falsifiability criterion. Behind it lay the desire to make a sharp distinction between deduction and induction, while at the same time purifying science of "metaphysical" elements: expressions that could not be empirically distinguished from one another (Zeus's activities from those of Yahweh).

It has turned out, however, that the approach does not perform the desired service. Consider the following statement by the logician Quine: "Any statement can be held true come what may, if we make drastic enough adjustments elsewhere in the system." [8] The point Quine is making is that one cannot describe the experiences that would refute some empirical generalization, without making quite a few assumptions about the nature of the world. If some unfavorable experiences begin to occur, the investigator need not reject the generalization; instead he may change these assumptions about the world. Much of the history of natural science that has been written in recent years has been devoted to showing the high frequency with which this latter reaction is adopted by scientists in this situation.[9] But as a consequence, the criterion of conceivable falsifiability has broken down. We start out with our clearly specified potentially contradictory evidence and no doubt feel very hard-nosed and realistic. But then when the contradictory evidence comes along, instead of bowing gracefully we reframe our situation without changing the hypothesis, so that a different body of evidence is now to be the contradictory of our hypothesis. This is by no means a peculiarity of soft science, and it has contributed importantly to the development of science. That is, one cannot dismiss the procedure of adjusting the theory to fit the facts as illegitimate. What is apparent is that the options for adjusting theory—and belief-systems—are greater than the falsifiability rule can handle.[10]

The fundamental message of the breakdown of falsifiability is the interaction between theory-belief systems and data, an interaction that is only partially mediated by induction. The reason the investigator is unwilling to accept the evidence is that he has other reasons for believing the hypothesis. These reasons are partly tied to the deductive body of theory from which the hypothesis came, some parts of which at least he believes because of their empirical status. Partly, also, they are tied to colligation, to the more informal and intuitive set of beliefs he and other scientists have about the way the world functions. These deductive and colligative reasons are treated by the investigator as if they were partial corroborations of the hypothesis, even though they contain no directly relevant data. To put it another and stronger way, there are three general types of verification procedures: verification by induction, verification by theory, and verification by colligation.[11] No one of them alone suffices to generate very high degrees of confidence in the correctness of a hypothesis, but all play a vital role in verification.

Walras, Heisenberg, and Velikovsky

These three gentlemen stand for three principles that in combination are extremely destructive of the econometric orientation toward verification in economics. We take them up in order.

Walras devoted his life to vindicating his father's thesis that scarcity is the key to understanding economics. Walras *fils* did this by developing the general equilibrium analysis which provides economics with what might be called its Fundamental Preconception: the proposition that everything depends on everything else. Of course each economic variable is dependent on others in a special way; the typical pattern of general equilibrium theory is that quantity variables, the amounts demanded or supplied, depend on the prices of all relevant goods and services. But the appearance of individual prices and quantities in several different equations of the whole grand system provides a much greater interdependence than this. And though many economists are not too enamored of the complex modern versions of Walras's theory, all of them accept the basic idea of ubiquitous and fundamental interdependence among economic variables. It is in this sense that economics has a Fundamental Preconception, too vague to be called a Fundamental Theorem, but a principle nonetheless on which there is consensus.[12]

Heisenberg is remembered as the father of the uncertainty principle in physics. It is less widely known that an idea in econometrics, the identification problem, is a very similar type of problem. We will explain it here in a special way by asking in effect, What would the uncertainty principle look like if it, rather than the identification problem, were what we faced in economics? Then the contrast between the physicist's and the economist's situation, with respect to verification, can be brought out more clearly.

Let us think of a very simple model of a market, in which the amount of the good demanded varies with the price of the good, and the amount of the good supplied also varies with the price. We can make a number of observations of actual price-quantity pairs representing actual purchases in various time-periods, and we want to use this information to find out what the supply and demand curves look like. To do this we are equipped with information on a third variable, income, which has a most peculiar property, namely that we can control its impact on the market. For example, if we decide to let income affect only demand, then when we observe our price-quantity-income triple, we can unequivocally identify the points as points on the supply curve. This is because the income variable is shifting the demand curve around with its variation, while the supply curve, not under the influence of a third variable, remains fixed, as in the figure. Similarly, if we set the income variable to affect supply only, we are able to discover the shape of the demand curve.

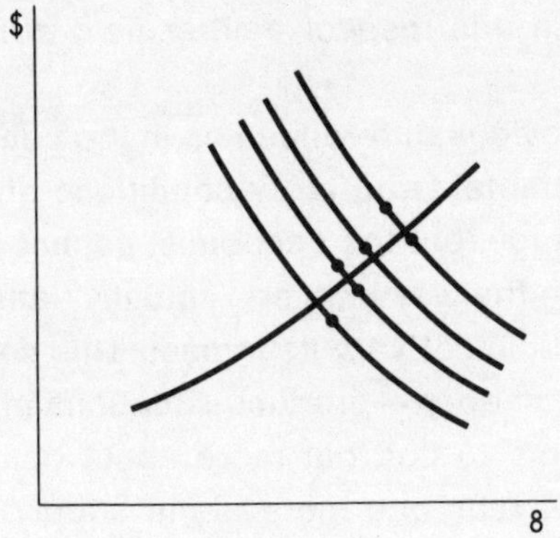

In each case we can find out only about one curve by taking these observations and are left in ignorance about the other curve. However, it is possible to let our income variable have mixed impact, putting say 20 percent of its weight on influencing the demand curve and the remainder on the supply curve. In this case we will find out just a little about the supply curve and quite a lot about the demand curve. But our principle of uncertainty sets strict upper limits to the total amount of information we can acquire jointly about the two curves. Thus, while working with this model, we are doomed to remain with a certain ineradicable amount of ignorance about what is going on, though we can control to some extent the area in which our ignorance is to be concentrated.

Roughly speaking, this is the way the uncertainty principle would work in economics. We are interested now in the differences that can be discerned in this model between physics and economics. But first, let us note a problem common to both fields, which is simply the possibility of error. In both disciplines observations may be incorrectly made or theories misapplied through ignorance or carelessness. In this respect neither field differs from the other.

The most obvious difference lies in the controllability of our income variable. Laboratory conditions give the physicist this advantage, but the economist cannot reproduce it. He is stuck with the way income "actually" affects demand and supply and cannot vary its impact. This constraint may —indeed, it often does—produce situations in which, so to speak, one wants to find out more about demand but the income variable tells one more about supply. There is no direct cure for this.

A second difference stems from the nature of theory in the two disciplines. The physicist's theory tells him that the uncertainty principle is built into the nature of matter; it tells him that this uncertainty cannot be avoided unless the theory that all physicists believe is fundamentally wrong. Theory tells the economist a very different story. The Fundamental Preconception tells him that he is wrong from the word "go" in his model. In fact, all economists believe that there are many more variables at work than are included in *any* estimated model. They are eliminated from consideration, not because they are believed to be irrelevant, but because, given the available data, their impact cannot be discerned. The real problem here is that the economist's theory has not done the job for him that the physicist's has: it has not provided him with an exclusive list of the relevant variables for his problem that he can put to work in the formal verification process. Instead, the economist is forced to tinker with his data and hypotheses until he can get the two to match up.[13] This violates fundamental canons of statistical inference, but is unavoidable so long as we are unable to specify our theories in such a way that they capture all the variables that theory tells us are relevant and for which we have enough data to be able to make valid inferences. And the Fundamental Preconception tells us that in fact we never *will* be able to develop such well-specified theories.

At first glance it might seem that this proliferation of causal variables is a blessing, rather than the bane it has just been claimed to be. For example, by adding a couple of well-chosen variables to our income model, we ought to be able to produce independent shifts in each curve—supply and demand—and so be able to observe them both after all. Something like this is in fact done in econometric work, the variables being chosen partly with a view to getting adequate identification. But there is a very serious flaw in this procedure. The flaw is that you cannot make the other variables go away by just ignoring them. If they really are causal factors in the problem, they are still operating, and identification by selection merely leaves the scientist attributing part of their effect to the variables he decided to include. In this case the econometrician is playing God without having first acquired the appropriate powers.

Now the Velikovsky principle must be added in. As discussed in earlier parts of this book, the Velikovsky principle says that the laws of economics (actually he was talking of physics, but we have transported him to an intellectually more hospitable climate) are not fixed forever, but change over time with the changing structure of society, and of man as well. In our market model it is now possible that income will at some point begin to affect supply and demand in different ways than it had done previously. Our observations may partly cover the old and partly the new way in which it acts. Theory provides us with no guidance here, nor does the Fundamental Preconception. The factors that can cause such change—ranging from wars, depressions, and sudden changes in foreign trade, to the longer-term and variable but powerful impact of new technologies, revolutions, etc.—are too diffuse and too poorly understood to permit their serious incorporation in a theory which could rationalize a particular econometric exercise.

The interactive effect of the three principles—the Fundamental Preconception, the uncertainty principle, and the Velikovsky principle—is substantially to weaken the theoretical case for econometrics as the most appropriate device for understanding the economy. Of course these qualitative arguments give no quantitative guidance as to how good or how bad the approach is. That can only come from a serious look at the quality of the results. The main point here is to illustrate the basic flaws in the methodology as applied to a subject like economics. These flaws seem to the author to imply that claims that econometrics represents the methodological ideal toward which the discipline should strive, are simply false.[14]

Verification by Theory

Over the years economics has probably attracted more than its share of practitioners whose orientation toward life tended to be pragmatic, realistic, even square. And yet the desire systematically to confront theory with fact has not been a notable feature of the discipline. As Blaug characterizes the discipline in historical perspective:

> No real effort was made to test classical doctrines against the body of statistical material that had been accumulated by the middle of the nineteenth century. . . . The endogenous variables manipulated in neoclassical models were frequently incapable of being observed, even in principle. . . . most of the theorems that emerged from the analysis likewise failed to be empirically meaningful.[15]

As one moves toward the contemporary scene the picture does not change much; Arrow, for example, uses rather similar language to describe the relation of Samuelson's corpus of neoclassical theorizing to the positivist criterion of meaningfulness, of empirical falsifiability.[16] One might argue that this is a major flaw in the discipline; no doubt it is, but the point should not be pushed too far, because it is not the central difficulty with modern economics. As the discussion of colligation indicated, a lot of work that looks like theorizing is oriented toward the verification of fact. This is a frightening notion for a positivist to accept, for it seems to open the door to endless and pointless metaphysical discussion which is entirely isolated from the problems which gave rise to and sustain the discipline. But it *is* true, and work of this kind has often been successful.

The Keynesian revolution offers some interesting insights into the kind of verification process through which a substantial novelty goes before it is incorporated into a science. Keynes's theory, after all, had a number of empirical implications, and some powerful policy-implications turned out to be verified. But the notable thing about both the *General Theory* and the massive discussion in the leading economic journals that followed its publication, is the dearth of empirical studies. Keynes himself put a note into the *Economic Journal* that contained four observations, of a sort, on changes in income and investment in the United States—one of which was unfavorable to his mulitplier theory, the others favorable.[17] Keynes considered this a favorable preliminary test of his theory. And this seems to be about as close as he got to systematically confronting the facts.

Perhaps the most widely cited empirical study of the early Keynesian years was one by Tarshis.[18] An important part of Keynes's argument for the ineffectiveness of wage policies in combating depressions was the claim that money wages and real wages moved in opposite directions. Money wages are very hard to reduce, and increasing them will lower real wages, which would be counterproductive. Tarshis ran an empirical test of the relationship and found that real and money wages had a strong tendency to move in the same direction. In the best anti-Popperian tradition, however, convinced Keynesians were unaffected in their views by this negative result; instead they revised the theory to make it consistent with this newly established fact and with its other implications. Direct empirical arguments are just not very effective in shooting down strongly held beliefs, because scientists in practice attribute corroborative value to their *theories.*

Given the importance which nearly all economists attached to ending depressions, one would expect that at least in the area of policy solid empirical work would play a central role in the development of Keynesianism. But this does not seem to be the case. To take just one example, consider the magnitude of the impact multipliers. Impact multipliers tell you how much change in the target variable you will get this year (or this quarter) from some given increase in the instrument variable; for example, how much GNP will increase this year if government spending is increased by a billion dollars. This is clearly a key policy variable because one wants to get the impact from an anti-depression policy as quickly as possible, and so to know at what level to set the policy variable so as to get GNP up without starting a runaway inflation. The standard textbook version (and early discussion) of Keynes did not attempt to isolate this change by estimating impact multipliers empirically. However, the technique for doing so had been developed by 1939, and there was enough data to at least make a preliminary stab at getting a useful result.[19] To the best of my knowledge, however, no one attempted to do this, and the first public presentation of estimates of impact multipliers of policy relevance does not occur until 1958, twenty-two years from the publication date of the *General Theory.*[20]

If economists were not seriously trying to relate Keynesian hypotheses to the statistical data, what were they doing? Well, essentially they were engaged in a series of rather abstract discussions, some of which hinged around the meaning of such key concepts as savings and the demand for money, and some of which involved the elucidation of the relation of the Keynesian theory to the previous classical theory and to alternative interpretations of the Keynesian theory. Economists were behaving as if the empirical situation—beyond the broad, vague outline of the facts known generally, if somewhat casually to all economists—was not significant until they got the conceptual situation straightened out and had reached some consensus on the nature of the key relationships among variables. The point was that statistical tests are of very little help in resolving controversies until there is general agreement on the properties of the surrounding theory. Without that general agreement, even tests that are accepted as decisive, as was the case with Tarshis, do not change anyone's mind. Of course, the typical situation is even worse, because tests which are generally accepted as establishing or refuting a hypothesis are quite rare. So much is impounded in *ceteris paribus* that there are always good reasons to hand for disbelief, provided one is sustained by some alternative system of beliefs.

The tremendous growth in econometric work over the last twenty years might suggest that the picture in economics has changed, and that now economists are more willing to accept the evidence of their statistical eyes. But this does not really seem to be the case. Partly, the increased quantity of work, to the extent that it does not simply reflect the increased number of professional economists, is a consequence of the vast increase in data and the consequently increased range of statistical tests that are deemed feasible. To a considerable extent it seems to reflect the convergence of views among economists regarding the background set of beliefs they hold in common, a convergence that has brought a wider range of problems to the stage at which relatively minor points of difference are at stake in an environment of substantial consensus. But the empirical support does not play a major role in fixing that common set of beliefs, the beliefs themselves are coming increasingly under challenge, and even the empirical testing that has been carried out has been disappointingly indecisive. We are entering an era when more complex and less precise criteria of verification than the positivist ones are going to play an increasing role in the actual practice of economics.

12

Storytelling

Storytelling is the output of the soft parts of economics. It is not taken seriously, in the sense that a formalist-positivist believes that the only parts of storytelling that are really a part of economics are the parts that can be formalized into the mathematical-statistical framework that is the positivist norm. The continued existence of storytelling as an approach to research by professional economists is thus viewed as a sort of prescientific remnant. But since no one wants to squabble over the definition of the limits of the science, and since there is still a demand for this type of product, especially in undergraduate teaching, there has been very little methodological discussion of the issue. The formalists are quietly confident that storytelling will die out as the older economists retire; perhaps many storytellers agree, or are at least afraid that this will happen, or even suspect that it may be a good thing.

If positivism were a correct philosophical position, and if the formalist tradition had generated a substantial body of hard results over the last two decades, the fate of storytelling would indeed be sealed. But these two tests have not been passed. So we had better look at this alternative method of generating results in economics and social science generally, to see what its strengths and weaknesses are and to appraise its survival value. Like most such methodological pictures, it is partly a description of practice, but partly a norm as well, because practice is somewhat idealized in our formulation. The method does not have prospects for becoming hard, but perhaps that is not a disadvantage; at any rate our description and appraisal will be as soft as the method itself.

Storytelling is an attempt to give an account of an interrelated set of phenomena in which fact, theory, and values are all mixed together in the telling. Historians of course are the archetypal storytellers, especially when the historian has some coherent purpose. He then tries to get the facts to fit his purpose, without misstating them. But much of the connective material for his story is not really factual historical material, but theory about human behavior, the impact of the environment on the actors, and so forth. This is woven into the story, and one of the major tests of storytelling historians is their ability to make the facts support the theory and vice versa.

The reader of a good story is persuaded. He appraises the various sections of the story partly in positivist terms ("What is the evidence in favor of statement X?"), but also in terms of its connections with other parts of the story that he believes to be true. Furthermore, there is a part-whole interaction in the corroboration process: if the whole story fits together, this is a verification "plus" for any particular essential part of it. This kind of interweaving of fact and theory in the story thus plays an important verificatory role, a role which is closely tied to what Whewell called colligation. A partly implicit set of beliefs is the glue that sticks the pieces of the story together, and that interrelates the parts to one another.

This account probably suggests that storytelling is methodologically primitive. True, in the harder natural sciences there is little use for such a procedure. But that is not to say that it is primitive, for the circumstances of interest to an economist are different; in particular, the economist must contend with that loser's combination, the Fundamental Preconception plus the Velikovsky Principle —that is, with a situation in which a large number of variables are relevant and in which there is an inherent paucity of data. To put it another way, it is not the method but the environment that is primitive. The method itself can be applied with great subtlety and can be very persuasive, but it is not always easy to explain exactly why a particular story is persuasive.

There is no question but that storytelling plays a greater role in those fields that were ranked low in terms of status in Chapter 1 than in those at the top, if one measures role in terms of the distribution of well regarded books and articles in these fields by method. But this is the case largely because of the distribution of pools of statistics and of formalizable problems which meet the formalists' tests, rather than because storytelling works less well in the upper reaches of the status-hierarchy of fields. That is to say, only storytelling is ubiquitous, and with good reason, because only with storytelling can one tie the research to the uses to which economics is put.

For instance, consider macroeconomic policy. A good

example of storytelling in this area is the annual report of the President's Council of Economic Advisors. At many places in the reports there are statements which are the result of careful econometric investigation. But these econometric investigations have a large component of adhockery built into their structure, an adaptation of the formal model to fit the needs of the story that is being told about the consequences of alternative courses of government action. These bits of adjusted formalism, however, are themselves tied together by stories, by plausible accounts of interactions and consequences widely believed for other reasons than that econometric study of them has been completed. And the whole report is an attempt to make the planned policies plausible by mixing together all the theories, facts, and even values, that the authors believe will carry some weight with readers.[1]

The way in which policy-oriented microeconomic studies are worked into the stories that form the actual basis of policy has been mentioned earlier. But perhaps more important are the economic stories that are not directly related to policy. These form the parts of economics that look most scientific in the special sense that they are oriented more toward generating understanding (equals instilling a belief-system?) than toward explaining what ought to be done about Problem X. There is, of course, a large implicit component in these stories, and often that is the most important part. Perhaps a very brief characterization of a story that seems very frequently to be told undergraduates will suggest the way storytelling tends to work these days in economics.

Judging from the textbooks, the microeconomics course required of economics majors in most departments of economics tells the following story. "The decentralized capitalist economy can and should be made to work well. Markets are most useful social devices in support of this aim because they allow people free choice in spending their incomes and selling their services for the income. Individuals are essentially mutually autonomous in their economic behavior and are strongly and primarily motivated by the desire for personal consumption and leisure. The capitalist productive system supports this orientation in many ways, both in its internal operation and in its reactions to consumer demands. There are some problems with capitalist productive régimes which center around the imperfections that may arise to inhibit competition among productive units, but the significance of these inhibitions is controversial. A well-functioning socialist economy would look pretty much like a capitalist economy, except that industry would be nationalized. Where interdependence between citizens and goods is strong, such as in defense, there is a case for government action, and governments do act in these areas. The most interesting aspect of income distribution is the way in which markets tend to provide income to individuals in accordance with the valuation placed on the individual's services by those who consume their fruits."

Only a few of these statements are actually to be found stated explicitly in standard textbooks. The rest are gotten across by the selection of topics and emphases. The reader of standard texts will find far less concern with the possibility of alternative interpretations that are fundamentally different in their implications than can be found in earlier neoclassical works of comparable aim, such as Marshall's Principles.[2] But then the *obiter dicta* tend to be formulated much more carefully too, so that the superficial appearance of bias is avoided. It is probably in this sense more than any other that economics has become more scientific during recent years. Of course the result of making such central parts of the story implicit is that these parts of the story are subject to only the weakest possible verification procedure. For many they seem plausible only because no questioning has been triggered during the course of instruction.

Some Properties of Storytelling

1 Suppose there was an island inhabited by a half-dozen whites and two or three blacks, and one wanted to know if there was any economic discrimination against the blacks. It is hard to believe that statistical decision-theory or formal modelbuilding would play any role at all in a careful study of this question. The investigator would want to bring with him a good knowledge of the ways in which economic discrimination may be practiced, and how it may be concealed. He would need a good ability to relate to all the people on the island, and he would need an open mind toward the possibility that some unique aspects of the problem would emerge from his study. Even the counting of instances of one kind of behavior or another would probably play a modest role. Single instances of behavior that were especially revealing of stable attitudes could easily count for more than sampling from some abstract population of events of the same kind, since the unique properties of each of the individuals would probably vitiate attempts to make instances similar enough for such enumeration to be of much interest.

Clearly, if the population of the island were ten thousand instead of ten, enumeration would count for a great deal more, and even econometric work would probably have some modest role to play. But this is because of the investigator's limitations: he cannot really get to know ten thousand people and the various ways in which each interacts with others. The use of formalist techniques is a second-best approach to this problem because the ideal technique is no longer feasible. Even on this big island, the old technique will count for a great deal, but that is not the main point. The point is that counting and modelbuilding and statistical estimation are not the primary methods of scientific research in dealing with human interaction: they are rather crude second-best substitutes for the primary technique, storytelling.

2 Stories tend to be unique. But then how can one have any confidence in them? The formal theory of statistical inference is built on the notion that the fewer instances you have the worse off you are, and that in the extreme case of a sample of one you have lost all ability to discriminate between degrees of confidence in your judgment on the hypothesis.

Going back to our island example, suppose there were ten small islands, all physically identical and containing the same population structure. Our investigators might still use open-ended techniques very profitably, but one would hope that there would be some careful standardization of many of their procedures, because one would certainly have greater faith in the results, particularly those ascribing causation, the larger the number of islands for which they seem to hold true. It looks as if we are back to the primacy of numbers and formalism, though at a different level.

There is only one trouble with this argument: it deals with an economic empty box. There are always unique features to an economic event which make its representativeness somewhat dubious. The islands will be different in important ways, and the experiences and capacities of the individuals will differ, and so on. Consequently enumeration is inevitably of the unlike, inference about the nonrandom and theory on the irrelevant. It does help to have more islands, but not nearly to the extent claimed in formalist methodology.

The heart of the bias against small sample situations in inference comes from the ignoring of colligation and its implicit verification by theory, among other things. As suggested above in Chapter 10, it is not enough to start with subjective probabilities as capturing this aspect of the process, because the subjective probabilities, in effect, are altered during the process of investigation. One begins to look at what one used to know in a new light, those subjective probabilities change, and the original formulation of the problem no longer fits by the time the investigation is over. For these reasons then, formalist methodology distorts the actual picture with respect to verification and creates a bias against (good) storytelling which is unwarranted.

3 Statistical decision-theory offers the investigator the opportunity to adjust his conclusions to his needs. That is, the same data may generate different conclusions depending on the use to which the results are to be put. For example, as previously noted, if one is very anxious to avoid falsely convicting the innocent, the same data may lead to a different conclusion than if one were much more anxious to avoid letting the guilty free. This flexibility looks rather like that which we were claiming for storytelling.

However, there are two important respects in which this is not the case. The first applies equally to subjective probabilities as noted above. It is simply that the problem often changes its nature during the course of the investigation, this change leads one to revalue the *a priori* information, and this interdependence plays an important role in judging the results. Storytelling is well adapted to introduce this phenomenon and appraise it as a part of the study, but the interdependence is not captured in statistical theory.

The second difficulty stems again from colligation. Such things as subjective probabilities and loss-functions are simply not the form in which our set of beliefs is available to us. There is no reason to believe that the unsystematic generation of such formalisms does any kind of a job in capturing the relevant aspects of the set of beliefs which influences the investigator's attitude toward verifiability of his hypotheses. Indeed, given the constraints of narrowness imposed by the data situation, they are almost certainly distorting of these beliefs. Again, the openendedness of storytelling allows the investigator to start from the language in which his "priors" are actually expressed.

4 An essential and unavoidable aspect of the formalist approach is the translation of the problem into formalist language. This largely eliminates all those aspects of the problem that are captured in the connotative richness of the participants' language. "To translate is to betray": this is no empty *mot*. Probably its impact is greatest in distorting and eliminating understanding of values, as will be suggested in Part V, but there are serious distortions stemming from the factual and theoretical sides as well. For example, a study of the prices paid by poor urban dwellers could give a very misleading impression if it concentrated on prices in stores which are basically fronts for various kinds of gamblers and pushers. And theories whose conclusions hinge importantly around such purely technical considerations as continuity or the paradoxes of the infinite are an example on the theoretical side. This problem is of course a commonplace, known to all formalists, but knowing about it does not remove the distorting bias. The risks of bias in storytelling are also great. But storytelling invites openendedness and the use of the most persuasive language; to this extent, the methodology itself provides a weaker stimulus to distortion.

5 It is indeed ironic that one of the great benefits formalism has conferred on economics is not the formalism itself but the pressure toward systematic storytelling. One remembers once again the reaction to programming studies in which the benefit they produce is appraised not so much in terms of the formal results as of the pressure toward systematic, goal-oriented collection of facts. A linear programming formulation then becomes essentially no more than the outline of a story one wants to tell. Best results are achieved when that is exactly the way in which one looks at the formalism, retaining perfect freedom to resort to information which will not fit the programming framework if it will help tell the story better.

On Verifying a Story

There is no well-developed methodology for doing this, given the intuitive and implicit nature of much of the process. About all we can do at this point is to offer a checklist of questions which must be given a serious answer as part of the story-verifying process. With the exception of the last two questions, whose inclusion will be defended later (Part V), the questions are the obvious ones:

1 Are the facts and theories correctly stated?
2 Are important facts or theories omitted?
3 Can one find other stories which use the facts and theories employed in the given story?
4 Are the facts and theories relevant or essential to the story; that is, can no other hypotheses be used to tell as good a story about the facts?
5 Do experts in the various parts of the story believe the story itself?
6 Are values correctly stated?
7 Are all relevant values included?

The stronger the "Yes" to each of these questions, the stronger is the verification of the story.

The work of formalists, whether theorists or econometricians, can play an important role in answering some of these questions. But that is only significantly true of the first two questions. Questions 3 and 4 are openended, their answer depending on the ability of the investigator to ferret out the considerations that are believed to be relevant to the issues. Question 5 is essentially an argument from authority, but of a peculiar form. One is asking the experts to judge the quality of an argument of which their expertise typically forms only a part, the reason for this of course being captured in the concept of colligation. The point is that the basic methodological element in economics, and all social science, is not the study but the story.

Why should anybody believe that the stronger the positive answers to these questions the more confident one can be, scientifically speaking, that the story is true? A case can be made; indeed, one is implicit in much that has already been said about method and the peculiarities of social science. But the main point is not really that this is how economists *ought* to behave. It is rather that this is how they do in fact behave; this is, roughly speaking, the methodology that we actually use in establishing our professional beliefs. Perhaps the science could be improved if we were more honest about this matter, for practitioners might then feel under less pressure to transform their studies into models of a procedure that has not worked and which really is not even believed. The result of that practice has been to sweep under the table some of the most important and profound issues that economics faces, as well as substantially to distort much potentially useful work.

Part V

Values and Deeds

13

Values in Economics

The lore of neoclassical economics tends to instill attitudes toward values in budding professionals which are rather roughly captured in the following set of principles:

1 Economics is a positive science. As a science it studies what has happened and what may happen, but not what should happen.

2 Of course each economist has his own set of values, and these influence his choice of topics and even his choice of research procedures. Such value-laden biases are inevitable. The only defenses against them are the scientific insistence on the spelling out of assumptions and procedures, plus the critical interest of those economists with other sets of values in this economist's research.

3 Every decision is based on a criterion, a set of values which provides the decisionmaker with the value-information needed to select the best alternative for him. These criteria may be studied positively by economists. For example it would be perfectly legitimate for positive economics to study the role that attitudes toward risk play in investment decisions.

4 When policies are being discussed scientifically, the economist starts by assuming some given set or sets of values and can then make his professional contribution, which is to analyze the consequences for each set of values of adopting alternative courses of action.

5 Efficiency is such a weak value, so widely believed to be desirable, that it can be treated as if it were a purely factual concept.[1]

6 It is usually convenient to assume that individuals are motivated by self-interest, and to give primary status to the tastes that capture this self-interest. Usually one also assumes that these tastes are stable, uninfluenced by the environment.

7 It is hard enough to make cardinal comparisons among alternatives: to find out whether an individual prefers one alternative much more than another. But to make interpersonal comparisons, to compare the relative states of two individuals, is really impossible. Such a comparison is no more than an opinion, over which there are likely to be great and essentially irreconcilable differences among any set of judges. This can of worms is best left out of economics entirely. The masters have set the tone for this procedure by writing very general "social welfare functions" which, in principle, capture the interdependence, and by then discouraging anyone from attempting closer specification by enumerating the very great and complex problems that lie in the way.

8 Welfare economics, the field which formally attempts to connect values and facts in economics, is uninteresting and pretty near empty of content.

Like all social sciences, economics has a great deal of trouble coming to terms with values. At the root of this difficulty, of course, is the positivist orientation. A neoclassical economist with methodological interests will in all likelihood subscribe to the emotive theory of value. This positivist view holds that values are the product of our emotions; this is what makes them unique to the individual and also what prevents them from being subject to change as a result of rational discussion. Hence their banishment from science. It is admitted that some profitable discussion about values is possible, but only when apparent differences in values are really based on differences about the facts. Then a reconciliation of views about the facts, a legitimate scientific goal, can lead to a reformulation of values. Even in this case the scientific discussion deals only with the facts and the logical consistency of the arguments.

The systematic pursuit of the positivist goal has led straight to the peculiar situation described in Point 8 above. Every economist knows how to write a social welfare function that, in principle, values complex alternatives in terms of some positive function of the utilities generated in each individual by the goods and services he receives or supplies. But no economist can think of anything useful to do with the thing once he has written it down. He knows that there are some problems with this notion of welfare; for example, if he wants it to be even marginally responsive to the wishes of the individuals included in the function, he will have to accept the likelihood that it will give him contradictory advice, telling him both that Alternative X is best and that Alternative Y is better than X. He also knows (Point 7) that there are no accepted techniques even for generating in a positive way these social welfare functions. At this point he probably throws up his hands and goes back to a more intuitive and implicit approach to values, so as to escape the criticisms that would be inescapable if he tried to spell the notion of social welfare out explicitly in any but the most abstract model.[2]

In some macroeconomic models, however (and in a few other places), the procedure of Point 4 is explicitly adopted. A model is presented that generates distributions of alternative feasible states of the economy that result from setting target variables, such as government spending and the supply of money, at various levels. A criterion is specified that tells how important are the relevant variables, such as the price level and the rate of growth of output, and how unpleasant it will be to get deviations from optimum values. Armed with this empirical model, one can study the effects on the criterion of believing in various moral values.

This represents a pinnacle of positivist achievement. If the model is a good one, anyone with normative interests can easily find out what ought to be done, by his lights, simply by telling the investigator which specification of the criterion is the one he believes in. The investigator switches the computer to "on," and in a few seconds the answer pops out: "This is what our policy-oriented friend should do: . . ." I think it is wholly fair to characterize the positivist ideal as a systematic attempt to provide situations just like this over as wide a range of economic problems as possible.

What sorts of objections can be made to this approach? There are at least five, most of which can no doubt be anticipated by anyone who has read this far.

In the first place, one cannot engage emotionally with

the criterion, and so the approach fails positivism's own test. For example, take someone who is deeply, emotionally affected by the misery that poverty causes. Then ask him to work through his emotional feelings about the optimal trade-off between unemployment and inflation. To engage in this rather complex and abstract task is to suppress rather than stimulate emotions. One can make a choice all right, but it is likely to be a "rational" choice, one which is based on "cool" judgments of political feasibility at least as much as on "hot" feelings for the state of the poor. This is not just a matter of the inappropriateness of the variables. The question is posed in a way which does not stimulate the emotions.

But the variables *are* inappropriate, and there is a systematic reason for this. The positivist, descriptive side of the problem dominates the model building. Having found a set of variables which have the twin properties that theory has something to say about their mutual connections and that an empirical basis for measuring them exists, the investigator then casts his eye about for a criterion. But the criterion has already been restricted in its arguments by the set of variables included in the model. There is no place in this scientific system for a serious discussion of what variables ought to be included in the model, because they ought to be in the criterion.

The positivist bias encourages suppression of value-laden variables. The parlous state of income-distribution theory is perhaps the best witness to this problem in neoclassical economics. Distribution can be brought in if it can be converted into an efficiency problem. The negative income tax becomes an interesting question for economists when it is posed as a choice among alternative ways of allocating some given sum of money among the poor. In this way the question of the optimal income distribution can be avoided, and where it cannot be avoided if included, it is simply excluded. Macroeconomic models provide the classic case of the latter tactic, and this despite the clear centrality of distribution to the problems of poverty and economic stability.

The variables of models constructed in such a way are inappropriate for yet another reason. There is a high degree of interdependence between belief-systems and behavior. The positivist approach keeps the value-aspects of belief-systems out of the arena of scientific discussion. When accompanied by a systematic bias in the tendency of the subject, as we have argued is the case in economics, such natural correctives to the bias in the belief-system as open and "serious" (i.e., professional) discussion of alternative beliefs are suppressed. Neoclassical economics produces neoclassical models, but perhaps not so much because the world works in a neoclassical way as because the minds of officially trained and approved economists work in a neoclassical way.[3]

Finally, this great positivist exercise does not work. To the best of my knowledge, there does not exist a single model of this type whose results are believed, in the sense that they are not first subjected to *ad hoc* revisions before becoming the basis of policy. What we have is not positivist science at work generating results about the real world in a policy-relevant way, but a series of methodological explorations which show no signs of converging toward powerful results.

Interpersonal Comparisons of Utility

Denial of the claim that one person can understand the relative satisfactions another person derives from different situations is a very central position in neoclassical economics. The reasons for this are quite varied. First, there is the fact that the neoclassical approach to human behavior, based on the assumption that each individual possesses a sort of map guiding him to choice over any bundles of goods and services that come his way, is indeed incapable of providing help. It has proved deeply inadequate to useful empirical work under the assumption of no interdependence of utilities; to attempt to do an even more sophisticated job with the tools of individual economic decision-theory would only emphasize this fact, which is papered over in textbook accounts by maintaining a very high level of abstraction in the discussion of consumer theory.

Another problem with interpersonal comparisons is that if they are accepted the liberal assumption of independent, autonomous individuals is unlikely to be sustainable. If you understand that I am deeply injured by your taking Action X as compared to Y, you may very well refrain from taking X even though you are marginally injured by Y. And if economists are forced to take such behavior into account, then all the fine optimality theorems about competitive capitalism are lost.[4] Closely related to this, is the loss of the individualist model—of the picture of man as an independent, autonomous entity, acting in an impersonal world. This image from the background world-view of liberalism can survive, at best, only modest doses of mutual interdependence. And so one finds that there are quite substantial reasons for finding it "convenient" to stay with analyses that do not seriously use mutual interdependence among individuals' value-systems.[5]

The web of preconceptions that has been built around this key bastion of neoclassical economics is very tightly drawn. Perhaps the best way to illustrate this fact for the reader, especially the neoclassical reader, is to offer a few stories which deal with various aspects of these preconceptions. None of the stories is decisive, but taken as a group they suggest the pervasiveness of interpersonal utility comparisons in society.

One of the striking features of economics textbooks is their concentration on trivial choices in discussing individual behavior. Perhaps the most discussed good in the textbook literature is the widget, a good whose properties are wholly under the control of the writer, whose significance for the consumer is marginal, a good for which the reader can have no basis for forming a view as to its desirability to others. In other trivial choices—coffee versus tea, or kidneys versus liver, to take the examples from Samuelson's text—one might easily believe he knows something about the tastes of those close to him, relative to his own, for these pairs of goods, and that that knowledge is correct and is held by most close friends or family members. But since the issue itself is trivial, the student can be led toward the static theory of consumer decisionmaking without feeling that some vital social factor in the problem is being ignored.

Strong emotions, rigidly avoided in discussions of the individual in economics, offer good opportunities to observe interpersonal comparisons clearly. I remember such an opportunity from my youth, involving a very strong emotion: fear. A number of us were cadets making a summer cruise on a sail-training ship. She was a full-rigged, three-masted ship, and one of the cadets' functions was to manhandle the sails from the rigging. Three of us were assigned to the starboard yard of the fore upper topsail, which was located some forty feet above the deck. Our first job was to climb the rigging up to the yard, walk out the yard on a footrope, and then, leaning over the yard, haul up the heavy canvas sail and secure it to the yard. This was not a very difficult task but was quite enough to trigger any latent fear of heights we might possess. Fear was not a fit subject for cadets to discuss, so there was no communication among us about how to organize for the job. However, it was immediately apparent to me that the three of us had very different attitudes toward the job. One cadet was eager to get aloft, his eyes dancing with pleasure; another was ambivalent, interested in the test of a fear of heights he did possess; and the third was very fearful and even appeared to walk in a somewhat flat-footed way toward the mast, as if seeking all the solid support he could find. These feelings seem definitely to have communicated themselves to the three of us, for we had no trouble whatsoever in forming a line in which the boldest, the first up, would go farthest out on the yard, while the most fearful was last up and remained closest to the foremast. There was no doubt in my mind as to the feelings of each of us—though I did not know the other two cadets very well—and our subsequent behavior seems to confirm the similarity in our individual appraisals of our relevant tastes. Interpersonal comparisons were made with sufficient accuracy to form a basis for social action.

Love is the emotion that, more than any other, promotes understanding of the desires of others, including of course even such trivia as tea versus coffee. In most normal people mere propinquity tends to generate such understanding, the amount of understanding no doubt being a positive function of the extent and duration of the propinquity. Much of our cultural life, most of all perhaps novels, promote through vicarious experience this kind of understanding of others. Surely the similarity in reactions of many people to many such exposures suggests that, at the very least, there is a central tendency to our ability to come to similar conclusions regarding the desires, the tastes, of others.

Economists are not without institutional support for their peculiar views about interpersonal comparisons. The market system itself provides a strong stimulus to these attitudes. For its central ingredient is the dividing up of choices in such a way that each act of choice, each purchase, has as little discernible impact on others as possible. This very act of division encourages a fragmented organization of information around the choice acts, which minimizes the individual's exposure to the cumulative effects of even his own set of choices. Most of the time the purveyors of a good are not significantly affected by one individual's decision to buy or not to buy. The individual's own interest in the decision, however, remains relatively strong. In this way, the market in effect biases the individual against taking any account of the effect on others of his economic behavior in the market place. The market system thus stimulates the adaptation of individuals to the economist's theory. But surely this is an argument against the market system rather than in favor of the economist's theory, a point which is reinforced when it is recalled that we are discussing welfare economics or the theory of evaluating the economy's performance.

The treatment of communication is yet another area in which economics has built up its defenses against interpersonal comparisons. The topic called "communication theory" deals only with the amount of information transmitted and received, without reference to content. Structural information theory takes account of the varying ability of the information to discriminate among different states of nature or events. But none of the theories deal with that fundamental aspect of communication, the development of understanding of oneself and others. This background—the world-view or image or network of commitments as it has been called—has been characterized by one economist, the founder of a great modern school of economics (whose followers, in this respect at least, are true epigones) as follows:

> So far from our knowledge of the consciousness of other persons being an "inference" from a "perception" of their behaviour, it turns out that the very capacity to perceive is developed through and dependent upon intercommunication between minds as conscious centers. . . . The common identification of "observed fact" with "sense data" is manifestly a confusion. The perception of an object rests upon ages of mental sophistication. Moreover, as we have previously remarked, no observation in the true sense is quite compulsory and unavoidable; no objectification will stand up under hard sceptical scrutiny; every perception of reality is more or less a voluntary act. Thought is saturated with purpose and concepts, emotion and metaphysical entities.[6]

Knight's point is made very nicely by Churchman, using an example from the economist's toolkit of discussions of measurement. Consider two people in different worlds who are in communication with each other. Each has a measuring rod and an object whose lengths they wish to compare. However, they have no objects in common, and so no basis for determining the relative lengths of their two measuring rods. Hence, goes the story, they will never be able to solve their problem. But, Churchman says, this is a very silly story. A tremendous amount of communication must have occurred for them to be able to make their difficulty mutually intelligible. The communication must have involved agreement on the meaning of a large number of terms and relations, and the establishment of common notions about the nature and stability of the worlds in which the actors dwelt, such as some considerable portion of the laws of physics and of biology (at least of the actors' own organisms). Given all this commonalty of experience, the search for a basis for comparison of length in the two worlds is a really trivial one. Churchman has here a beautiful parable of the trivialization of social thought brought about by the denial of the power of language and communication, which in economics is closely tied to the inculcated gentlemen's agreement to ignore interpersonal comparisons.[7]

The reader who has not had much exposure to economists' reasoning must be rather nonplused by this chapter. The idea that we do know something usable, something "publicly testable," about the belief-systems of other people, must seem rather banal and obvious. But that is not at all true of economists, and I rather doubt that their belief in the efficacy of independence-magic will be easily shaken, whether the argument concentrates on the absurdity of the assumptions or the weakness of the conclusions or the irrelevance of the theory to current policy-issues. We have said little on the last point, but here the problems are obvious even to economists. The issue of manipulation of individuals through socialization by family and school and profession and media simply cannot be discussed in terms of a model that does not admit the possibility of such manipulation. Externalities, the problems of environment that cannot be solved by relying on the market, call for social action and for the kind of interdependence that supports the understanding and implementation of good solutions; probably a major instrument of adaptation to externalities will prove to be changing the understanding of their environment by humans and the developing of feelings of awareness of these direct effects as a basis for individual as well as collective decision. This sort of orientation cannot be simply tacked on to current neoclassical theory, because an entirely different notion of the nature of man is implicit in it.

14

Five Ways of Looking at "Ought"

Suppose a naïve positivist, turning for the first time from the study of facts to values, asked himself what the criterion of meaning for a value might be. Remembering (see p. 160) that, in his philosophical credo, the meaning of an empirical assertion is determined by the experiences that would refute it, he might well come up with its precise ethical analog: the meaning of an asserted rule of obligation is determined by the experiences that would refute it, that is, by the experiences which, if they occurred as a consequence of accepting it, would lead one to reject the rule of obligation. Well, why not? As we have seen, facts, observations, are not nearly as hard as the logical positivists once thought, and the process of verification is far fuzzier than formalist economists tend to claim. At the same time, the social, as opposed to individual, nature of man suggests that values may be somewhat less personal and subjective than a positivist would claim. In the present chapter we discuss alternative ethical positions with a view to supporting our naïve positivist's view of ethics.

"Ought" from "Is"

Several years ago a discussion was initiated in a philosophical journal over the relation between simple factual statements and value-statements.[1] The instigator of this discussion argued that it is possible to derive a value-statement as to what one ought to do from a set of purely descriptive statements. The discussion has continued over the years and has not yet quite exhausted itself.[2] A simple example of the type of argument involved is the following: Doing A will produce pain. Apart from producing the pain resulting from A, doing A will have the same consequences as not doing A. Therefore A ought not to be done.

At first glance, this seems a most peculiar argument to occur in a professional journal of philosophy. Ever since the ancient rhetoric texts, the idea of analyzing arguments in ordinary language by introducing implicit premises to close the system logically has been accepted procedure. All that is needed in the above example is to recognize that implicit premises abound in ordinary discourse and to add the necessary implicit value premise: Other things equal, one ought not to produce pain.

Are editors of philosophy journals really as desperate for material as this? No, not quite; rather the explicit topic under discussion served as a sort of screen for discussion of a rather different question. This discussion has to do with the performative aspects of language, with the connotative urge to action that accompanies many denotatively descriptive statements in ordinary language. The contemporary version of this discussion was initiated by Wittgenstein, though it has historically long philosophical roots.

And the idea here is not so simple. Roughly speaking, it is that a great deal of meaning is imbedded in this performative aspect of language, that it is not clear that one can separate the performative from the descriptive aspects without distorting at least the former, and that in particular, attempts at logical or syntactical separations are especially distorting of meaning.

The argument as just stated does not seem to be in dispute, though various formulations of aspects of it have been offered. By and large, dissent has been restricted to asserting the ability, in principle, of an analyst to find implicit premises which will carry the argument without violating Hume's Guillotine, the strict separation in logic of value and factual statements. But if one accepts the performativist thesis that words are deeds, one's views on the principle of locating implicit premises make relatively little difference. The central problem of understanding such language is no longer to distinguish the formal syllogisms on which it is based but to understand the ways in which words and phrases are being used. This is much less a question of logical analysis than it is appreciation of the richness of the language and possession of experiences requisite to such understanding. Logic is in the background, fact and value are intertwined, and understanding is the desideratum.

Perhaps the best-known example of an apparent ought-from-is argument is the so-called Brandeis Brief, an argument before the Supreme Court on the constitutionality of a ten-hour-day law for women.[3] The brief consisted of a very short statement arguing that such a law was consistent with the principles of the Fourteenth Amendment, such as the right to equal protection from the laws. This was followed with a very detailed description of the conditions of women and other workers in the relevant industries. The presumption of the brief seemed clearly to be that one could derive the short value-statement from the long factual analysis.

Again it seems bootless to seek some logical formula which will provide formal closure to such an argument. The basic notion was very simply that any reasonable human being possessing the normal capability to imagine what it was like to try to live under the described circumstances would agree that for the government to regulate the situation was not per se a violation of equal protection or due process. The centrality of the need for protection depletes any cogency these principles might possess for the issue. The real difficulty here is not so much that the lawyer is trying to derive ought from is, as that means and ends are being mixed because of the apparent insertion of descriptive statements into a criterion of choice. To this problem we turn next.

Means and Ends

Teleological ethics has dominated economics since Adam Smith. The idea that means and ends are distinct forms the basis for the positivist approach and for the distinction between criterion and environment in decision theory. Behind the formal structure of economics lies an attitude toward ethics that is essentially teleological, because of the economist's inextinguishable interest in trade-offs, in appraising situations in which you always have to pay a price of some kind to get something you want. All over social science, and perhaps all over modern life, teleological orientations have tended to dominate because of the ubiquity of problems which seem to be presented to us in this form.

This is not to say, however, that experience shows that this is a natural way to look at human problems. In fact, there seems to be a great difficulty in discussing problems, and so presumably in solving them, in a way which strictly preserves the enjoined separation of fact and value. Rare indeed is the teleological philosopher who has not been accused of confusing the descriptive and the normative. As we have seen many economists have suffered the same difficulty in forming attitudes toward Pareto optimality.[4] Indeed, economists have tended to try to formulate anything they wish to discuss in a descriptive language regardless of its ethical content (remembering the warring tribes parable of Chapter 10).

Consider, for example, the notion of efficiency. One can still find economists saying that efficiency is simply a relation between physical variables and has no normative implications.[5] But in application it is a very different thing. The value-judgment here comes in when one classifies variables as inputs or outputs. This is not an arbitrary process at all, as will be suggested by thinking a moment about the status of labor. If some kinds of labor are indeed satisfying, then increasing the opportunities for performing that kind of activity might very easily be thought of as of a piece with increasing the rate of more conventional outputs. One would then want to classify that labor as an output. The classification is based on a preliminary—and almost entirely implicit—judgment as to what is valued and what disvalued in a society. Efficiency is too important to economic analysis to be treated as a norm without seriously damaging the positivist status of the discipline.

The Gross National Product concept is one in which the distortions of means-ends separation has produced an even more distressing situation. Analytically, GNP is a criterion, a measure of how well the economy is performing. As such the concept, and no less its constituent parts, has serious flaws. It is not too much to say that the likelihood that an increase in measured GNP will be accompanied by an increase in the welfare of the population has never been seriously appraised.[6] The reason for this is very simple. To do so requires that values be discussed, and that is not a serious activity for a professional economist. The consequence of this attitude is also very simple. A flawed concept has continued to be used for years without any within-discipline pressures to improve its moral quality. The means-ends separation effectively suppresses a much-needed line of investigation.

Usefulness of the means-ends separation depends to a great extent on the existence, for the individual at least, of general principles of judgment which can be converted into the specific criteria which are used in actual decision-making. Unfortunately, however, about the only major conclusion that emerges from the two-and-a-half-millenium tradition of ethical philosophy is that such rules are nonexistent. To take an example that has been the subject of much recent discussion, consider Hare's rule of universalizability.[7] This variant of the Kantian imperative says that moral judgments, to be valid, must be made to cover the behavior of all people in similar circumstances. A moral judgment is then a prescription enjoining a certain kind of behavior which everyone is assertedly obliged to comply with in the given set of circumstances. It is hard to dispute this claim, provided a suitable definition of "similar circumstances" is provided, but of course that definition is never forthcoming in ethical argument. The result, in this case as down through the history of philosophy, is a noble statement with little or no guidance as to how to convert it into a usable criterion of choice.

Sen has put the matter in a slightly different way. After surveying the major proposals of economists as to rules for setting up criteria of social choice, such as Pareto optimality and majority rule, Sen concludes:

> What this result possibly reveals (as do other results in the book) is an important difficulty in postulating general conditions in collective choice rules, viz, these conditions are essentially opaque. It is easier to secure acceptance of these conditions than the acceptance of all their implications.[8]

The problem is thus that the known rules for collective choice are not universalizable, even though they are at least close to being applicable to choice. They are also not generalizable in a different sense from that above: one cannot in conscience say that the collective-choice rule will work in a wide range of situations, even though one *can* specify a limited range of circumstances in which a given collective choice rule produces good results. But this does not really help, for it says that the appropriate collective-choice rule must be derived from an analysis of the situation, in which case one can only specify the choice rule after one has analyzed the specific situation. Since we have no specific guidance from universalizable rules to determine to which class of situations our situation is to be called similar, we cannot in fact perform that initial analysis.

There is considerable practical experience in economics with a rather formal application of a means-ends system to decisionmaking. This is the business-and-government application of linear (and nonlinear) programming. The criterion is specified—as precisely as can be—in the form, for example, of the sum of the costs of the various components of the problem. The environment is specified in a set of constraints, setting, say, minimum expenditure and activity levels for the various parts of the program. The formal solution then consists of calculating by a sophisticated and powerful routine the levels of the set of activities that minimizes cost, as measured by the criterion. Literally hundreds of such problems have been set up and solved in modern industry and government all over the world. The results have certainly been positive, in the sense that costs are very often shown to be reducible by anything from 5 to 20 percent and more.

Nevertheless, practitioners have frequently encountered problems that are the practical manifestations of the abstract issues we have been raising. Programmers in business are often confronted by the businessman who expects to be told what he is supposed to be maximizing or minimizing: he expects guidance from the technical consultant, not in the positivist sense of how to find the best means to his established ends, but advice as to what his ends should be. It is not at all that the businessman is indecisive; it is rather that it is not really natural for him to think of problems within this strict means-ends conceptual frame.

A second aspect of programming is captured in the slightly cynical but nevertheless accurate slogan "Nobody believes the results of this stuff, but it is often worth doing because it forces the decisionmaker to have data systematically collected and examined." The problem here is partly that the structure imposed on the problem by the mathematical formulation is known to be imprecise (for example, the constraints in practice are rarely as rigid as specified in the problem and the criterion doesn't really have the specified form); but at least as important is that a good deal of information is available about both criterion and constraints which cannot be fitted into the formal problem. This information leads to the usual practice of *ad hoc* adjustment of the results before they are applied in practice. Again it seems that the means-ends dichotomy is not the way in which people typically approach decisions.

Rule Utilitarianism

At the opposite extreme from the means-ends dichotomists lie those variously called "deontologists" or "rule utilitarians," who hold that moral prescripts have the form of simply enjoining actions, of classifying actions into two boxes labeled "right" and "wrong." There is no means-ends dichotomy here because there is no appeal to the consequences of an action in judging its rightness. And this of course implies that there is no problem of balancing one right against another, of trade-offs.

Judging from a very cursory search, the last notable economist to espouse such a position was William Godwin, and for obvious reasons. It may be that rule utilitarianism can in principle be made equivalent, or translated into a means-ends language.[9] This can be done in principle because every conceivable act can certainly be put in one or the other of the two boxes. But the same problem emerges here as in the case of universalization of teleological values: no one has ever managed to specify right acts in an appealing way with any degree of detail.

To what extent are the difficulties we attributed to means-ends arguments attributable to the practical use of deontological ethical forms? Probably such norms are very widespread as ethical rules of thumb. Much of one's purchasing of goods is habitual and is concretized in terms of formally deontological rules, such as "I ought to get a half dozen loaves of bread" or "I should avoid buying a car with a high compression ratio." But these rules are not very basic; it is just that one does not anticipate any conflict of values which will call them into question, and so a strict injunction is simply the most convenient form of storing one's practical ethical views with respect to many choices. This applies to the behavior of individuals in large organizations as well as to their consumption behavior.

However, from time to time rules of this kind are called into question by changes in the environment. The above rule for automobile purchase is probably of quite recent vintage for many who hold it today. When such questioning of a deontic rule begins, then a genuine conflict of values has arisen which inevitably takes one into the realm of appraisal of values. One might think that this forces one back to a teleological position of measuring trade-offs. Assuming that the individual is not mistaken in his values, this will be true if there is indeed a stable and unchanging value system possessed by the individual, to which reference is to be made in revising the rules of thumb. However, this latter position is very weak, as we have seen. No one seems to be able to get within striking distance of a useful specification of that stable, basic value-system. Again we are in the position of having only unspecifiable generalities to guide us in making specific choices.

Marxism

As a system of thought Marxism has never been constrained by positivist ethics. The Marxist position that there are objective values has opened up the possibility of using normative concepts in positive analysis and of discussing these concepts in terms of both their positive and normative implications. The notion of surplus is such a concept. Banished from neoclassical economics for more positive notions such as savings and investment, at least partly on the grounds that one cannot discuss surplus without discussing such essentially value-laden ideas as necessary consumption, surplus has thrived in Marxism. The positive and normative are thoroughly mixed in this notion, which implies not only a definition of socially necessary consumption but—in most applications—also of waste. There are no methodological bars to attempt empirically to estimate such values within the Marxist frame of reference.

The notion of exploitation illustrates the fundamental nature of the mixing of fact and value in Marxism even more clearly. Think of a nineteenth-century coal-mining town with its grimy broken men and stunted children down in the village set among the slag heaps, while the coal baron relaxes in his villa in the bosom of his healthy family. Even in this bathetic caricature one can feel the reality in the concept of exploitation. The descriptions of this sort of life in Marx and Engels and the Hobsons provide a basis for the notion of the extraction of the surplus through control of the means of production, and simultaneously generate horror and revulsion in the reader. At least in its clearest-cut applications, there is no more powerful justification of interweaving norm and description in economic literature than this.

The advantage offered by interweaving fact and value so completely is that investigators are encouraged to deal with all the major aspects of a problem, rather than concentrating on those issues that are formally acceptable to the positivist canon and convertible into puzzles. Since normative elements seem quite inescapable in social analysis, it is surely preferable to have them integrated into the science, given only that that is feasible.

Marxists, however, have not really escaped the major difficulties that confront any attempt to integrate values with facts. Even if one agrees with them that this is desirable, or goes farther and suggests, as does Boulding, that facts and values are formed by very similar processes,[10] one still does not yet have any useful rules of procedure for generating and especially for verifying hypotheses having a strong value-content. Marxists are always appealing to the laws of dialectics for guidance, but as Cornforth points out: "Investigation of universal laws of dialectics remains an open field. It is something that has been projected but not yet systematically done. And the laws that have been written down. . . . still lack both the precision of formulation and the systematic derivation to be expected of anything that can rank as science." [11] Marxism, too, despite success in some particular places, has not provided a usable solution to the problem of integrating fact and value within a scientific framework.

Situation Ethics

If there is a theological version of the Critique of Practical Reason these days, it is situation ethics.[12] This particular manifestation of the pragmatic and eclectic in ethics has grown up in both Germany and the United States since the war. The basic notion is that what one ought to do emerges from a close involvement in and study of a particular situation. It is the moral equivalent of our management consultant's view of business decisions (Chapt. 7): "You worry about the problem for awhile and then you change." In situation ethics you are faced with a moral dilemma (in practice, not in the abstract); you concern yourself with understanding your situation; and in time you come to know what you ought to do.

The eclectic nature of this approach is clear. General principles of conduct, of right action, will play a role at times, as will a study of the probable consequences of the relevant actions. But one does not start out with these rules, rather the situation is presumed to provide one with a basis for judging which rules are relevant and which are not. Facts, too, play a central role, for it is the study of the facts that is to reveal the relevance of alternative moral principles. Past experience also serves its role, not only in suggesting alternative principles, but in providing implicit guidance as to how rules can be correctly selected in a given situation.

The very eclecticism of this approach reduces the impact of the problems which are attached to the ethical approaches already described. And the use of such pragmatic bases of decision as the lessons of experience as to the emergence of notions of right from the interaction of all relevant considerations seems to strip the objector of any basis for criticism.

Nevertheless some doubts remain. The advice, "Inform your conscience and then let it be your guide," is surely unexceptionable, but there is no guarantee that you are correct, other than the judgment of your conscience. Without some evidence to the contrary it might even be argued that the informed conscience makes systematic mistakes of ethical judgment, and the defenders of situation ethics do not attempt to collect evidence on the performance of the conscience when applied in a manner they deem appropriate. There is no problem with the specificity of the rules of procedure in situation ethics—everyone can do it. The problem is, there is no accumulation of evidence as to the similarities in individual interpretations of these rules, or of the relation between application and performance. One seems to be back with the intuitionists, with a claim that a rule works, and that all you need to do to believe this is to give it a try.

Conclusion

Our very brief survey of approaches to values has suggested that there are serious problems with the neoclassical approach, that there is some promise in alternative ethical systems, but that each alternative in turn has its own difficulties with which to contend. At several places in the approaches discussed in this chapter, it is asserted that correct or valid values can be found, but nowhere is the procedure spelled out in a way which suggests that anything like a scientifically satisfying procedure has been found. The ingredients required for a good scientific theory of values include at least the following:

1 The language used must be capable of comprehending in analysis both the descriptive and performative aspects of expression.

2 It must be capable of conveying complex understanding of situations.

3 Formulations must be fairly close to actual behavior so as to be both a genuine guide to action and a bearer of the connotations which are embedded in descriptions of the situation.

4 The process of solution must be tied to a social system, so that public testability of the results is assured.

5 The procedure must be capable of taking account of changing values, both during the decision process and over collections of decisions.

We turn now to a procedure that, in some of its applications, meets all of these criteria.

15

ooooooooooooooooooooooooooooooooooooooooooooooooo

Law as a Moral Science

The neoclassical social welfare function is an attempt to provide economics with a means of bringing interpersonal comparisons of utility to bear on policy decisions. No branch of economics has as generally accepted a claim to failure as welfare economics, the branch of economics in which constructing social welfare functions lies. Most economists seem to take this failure as evidence that interpersonal comparisons cannot be made with the precision required by policy decisions. The main argument of this and the last two chapters is that this particular failure of economics is merely a failure of approach, and that there does exist an established and successful scientific procedure for making interpersonal comparisons.

Law as a Kuhnian Science

In Part 1 neoclassical economics was appraised by means of the half dozen properties which Kuhn has argued are necessary, and perhaps sufficient, for the existence of a science, viewed more as a social system than in terms of its epistemological commitments. On that basis it was clear that economics meets quite well these criteria, which were established originally from a study of the history of natural sciences. We now apply the same rules to law, defining the field so as to make the fit as close as possible to the Kuhnian standard:

1 The first test is the existence of an invisible college defined in terms of commonalty of training and of the network of professional interactions. Law, as a system of science, revolves around the work of appellate courts. The decisions of these courts, including of course in the United States the supreme courts at both the state and federal level, are the ones that make their way into the texts, commentaries, and casebooks that are the lifeblood of the legal profession. The judgments of these courts are taken as the primary basis for the precedent system of judgment in the making of current decisions, and are the ingredients on which budding lawyers are trained. Interconnections are thus established, at least within the American judicial system, among appellate judges, academic lawyers, and practicing lawyers, which provide the system of interactions required by the invisible college concept. One might think of the scientists of this system as consisting of appellate court judges, the lawyers who frequently argue before them, and the academic commentators whose writings are read by this group, with other members of the profession serving, functionally speaking, as apprentices, research assistants, and the like. But there is no real need to dichotomize. Lawyers, like other scientists, are given a careful indoctrination in the appropriate set of commitments in the better law schools, all of which have a common approach to the law and its practice and which tend to use similar procedures and texts. Out of this training a set of lawyers emerges, some fraction of whom, as in all other sciences, end up making contributions to the science of law. The invisible college functions very effectively in law.

2 Law tends to be organized on a national basis; consequently one might question whether the requirement that the invisible college be concerned to solve problems about the behavior of nature is met. Other social sciences, though the national component tends to be much stronger than in natural science, nevertheless have a strong international component, none more so than economics. But though an American lawyer may frequently cite British precedents in his briefs, he is less likely to go to Continental experience, much less still farther afield. This sort of parochialism is definitely a weakness in the case for law as a science, though we will return to its defense below.

3 There is no doubt that the problems on which lawyer-scientists work are typically problems of detail. The overwhelming emphasis on the case approach, not only in the decision process but even in instruction, insures a continuing emphasis on just this aspect of the subject.

4 Despite appearances, it is true that lawyer-scientists themselves define the problems and the nature of acceptable solutions. One might think that the function of legislative statutemaking, with its strong extra-legal membership, contradicts this assertion. But this is to mistake the function of the law as conceived by lawyers themselves. The law, including statutes, is taken as given, as exogenous data to legal science. Law's function begins with the interpretation of statutes, not with their construction. And lawyers accept only their own interpretations as to what are relevant problems in this area. True, a legislature may step in and define the relevance of a particular statute more precisely than in the past. When it has done so, the act is treated by the legal profession as the operation of a sort of shift parameter: Given this new information, how is one to interpret the statute? Statutes are not endogenous to the legal system. Once this is accepted, the primary responsibility of lawyers to the members of their invisible college in defining procedures and solutions follows immediately.[1]

5 The range of subjects of interest to the science is also under the control of the invisible college. Of course, an appellate court is required to respond in some way to every appeal that is made to it, and this is a considerable constraint on its activity. Nevertheless, the court is free to decide that the issue raised is irrelevant to its operation. Furthermore, academic lawyers have the kind of freedom traditionally held by scholars to write on whatever subject they wish, subject to traditional scientific constraints on relevance imposed by the scientific social system, such as editors' and referees' opinions. For the courts, though it is true that the judicial social system requires consideration of all appealed cases, the reactions of the judges is basically subject to the constraint of collegial approval or disapproval.[2]

6 The system of legal problems of interest to the profession as defined above is clearly self-sustaining. As long as human conflict persists, the uniqueness of individual conflicts continues to pose new issues of law, which are not reduced by the achievement of a valid formula for dealing with any single class of cases. Legal systems, like most other sciences, die out only when they are suppressed.

The appraisal suggests that the legal system meets to a surprisingly high degree the standards set by Kuhn for the existence of a normal natural science. Perhaps the weakest link in the argument is in the interaction between legislation and judicial action, but even here the separation of the two actions into distinct social systems suggests that the consequent diminution of freedom of scientific behavior is minimized. And the national parochialism is weakened by the similarities in conclusions reached by these semiautonomous legal systems.[3] Basically, law has the properties required for a functioning scientific system of truth-seeking.

The Problem of Legal Science

The fundamental problem that legal science is asked to decide is, What is the nature of one man's obligation to another? The situation calls for interpersonal comparisons of a kind very similar, at times identical to those captured so fruitlessly in the social welfare function. It is a question of who gains and who loses, and in civil actions almost never of finding a situation in which all may gain. Thus the problem posed is one of genuine dilemma, of human conflicts, and of the demand that they be resolved justly.

Philosophers and social theorists have proposed descriptions and definitions of the nature of law for centuries in a tradition fully as rich as that of political theory. The solution to this question posed above is by no means the only possible one, and so there is some need to defend its choice, however briefly, against some leading alternatives.

Consider, for example, a well-known case in administrative law in which the question under appeal was whether or not newsboys were employees of a newspaper company and so under the Wagner Act rules governing collective bargaining.[4] One might think that this was simply a question of fact, of testing the legally established definition of "employee" against the actual relationship of newsboy and publisher. But this was not the way the case was actually decided. For example, the judge took into account, accepted as germane to the case, information such as the extent to which the relevant newsboys were heads of families, a consideration which seems clearly related to the welfare implications of this decision rather than the simple question of accordance with definition. It was the judge's belief that such facts were relevant in view of his own obligation to interpret the intent of existing law. That is rather more than simply establishing a question of fact.

A positive or noncognitive theorist of law might argue that the legal function is not to consider obligation at all, since moral questions are without meaning. Instead, the lawyer and judge have as their task to understand the law in a positive way as a set of statements. Thus our judge in the newsboy case uses intent to be sure, but he does so by studying such background as the history of the passage of the relevant law. His own job is simply to formulate the facts in such a way that it is possible to put this case in one of the two wholly positive boxes: "employee" or "not employee." But this takes no account of the development of law and of the judicial role in that process. In Anglo-American law it is easy to isolate judicial decisions that are landmarks in the development of the law itself and which cannot be related in any but the most indirect way to past legal decisions or statutes. In any landmark decision the judge does a good deal more than categorize positively.

Judge Hand was a proponent of the view that the judge was engaged in a process additional to that just mentioned. He was obliged to consult "the generally accepted moral conventions current at the time." His judgments do not in fact appear to be based on any careful empirical tests in accord with this standard, and one is led to suspect that this formula is just one of many applied by judges who do not wish to state baldly that they are bringing in their own moral valuation as an element in their decision process.[5] Of course the proponents of "sociological" theories of law hold that courts have the obligation to do precisely this, even at times to the point of inserting values that conflict substantially with current moral conventions, if they are deemed socially desirable on some overriding grounds.

The appellate court is thus engaged in a highly creative process of determining the nature of mutual obligations in situations where, often enough, one man's gain is another's loss. The court is constrained in its judgments by existing statute, past precedent, and the accidents which bring particular disputes before it. But these constraints are far from sufficient to prevent the court from making moral judgments; in fact, their actions seem steeped in moral judgment.

Verification in Law

As described above, law seems to fill the gap which pervaded the ethical approaches of the last chapter: their inability to get from general rules to application in the specific instance. The court has a large set of appropriate rules already prescribed for it; it faces a specific case and is required to make a judgment. The whole elaborate apparatus seems to function primarily for the purpose of making this connection.

How well does it work? This job requires the making of moral judgments. Can they be verified with any confidence? That has always been the rub with putative objective theories of value, that they provided no mechanism for verifying in a scientific manner the results application of the rules in the hands of any given investigator would produce.

The verification process in law is quite well developed. There are of course the procedures developed for conducting trials and the making of appeals which are direct checks on the performance of the trial courts. These are the legal counterparts of the tests applied in research by individual investigators and teams in all sciences. This does help greatly to standardize the process by which results are reached and to ensure that the decision is made in full knowledge of the possibly relevant facts, but it is not in itself a verification of the decision.

This latter step comes through the processes of development of law itself. Tort law, which is largely judge-made law in the United States, affords one of the strongest examples of the verification process. There are fifty-one relevant jurisdictions, each with its own judicial system, each with an autonomous (but highly interdependent) tradition of law behind it. Nevada courts are under no obligation to accept decisions of the California Supreme Court; nevertheless, they are highly likely to consult at least key decisions made by that body in considering their own cases. The test of an obligation asserted in one of these jurisdictions is the extent to which the doctrine spreads to the other jurisdictions as relevant cases come before them. Furthermore the interests of litigants tends to insure that a decision of this kind does come to the test in other jurisdictions. When a doctrine has come to be accepted generally throughout all these jurisdictions, it has been subjected to a testing whose care exceeds that applied by economists to all but the most studied facts.

Does this process differ in any essential way from the process by which facts are verified in science? If it does, I cannot locate the peculiar feature. The investigator—that is, the appellate judge, assisted by lawyers representing the litigants and the trial court's findings—has immersed himself thoroughly in the empirical facts of the situation, has surveyed the relevant historical record of similar cases, has studied the various principles of obligation that have been deemed relevant to cases of this type, and has tested each against the above facts, selecting that one which is most closely consonant with past rules for judgment, while taking due account of the uniqueness of the particular case and the needs of justice. This ruling is then subject to frequent further tests in other similar cases, using the same techniques, in some of which of course the courts are required to give heavy weight to this ruling, but many of which are not. After all this, lawyers are likely to refer to the principle stating the specific obligation as "valid," which is at least a clear indication of how they view the process in practice.

On what basis might one disagree with this finding? After all, nothing is more common than for citizens to claim that the courts have done them an injustice. Given that they are referring to the above process and not to the decision of some jury or trial judge, one might say something like the following.

A citizen who is not familiar in a detailed way with a considerable number of similar cases is not in a very good position to make a judgment. He is very likely to be mistaking some specific aspect of the question for the most relevant one, a problem which would become apparent to him if he were more familiar with this type of problem. Alternatively, a citizen who was not familiar with the various attempts that have been made in the past to apply other principles of obligation to problems of this kind is similarly ill-equipped to make the judgment, because he has not yet opened his mind sufficiently to the range of possible solutions and the problems that accompany each. If the citizen passes both these tests, then he has standing as a critic of the decision. To allow him such standing before these two tests were passed would be roughly like letting the dictator enunciate the laws of genetics, if not quite so dramatic in its consequences. In other words, there is a clearly specifiable expertise which must be acquired before one is qualified to make these moral judgments in a plausibly correct way.

Examples of this verification process abound, but perhaps the most striking instance in recent years comes from the development of third-party liability doctrine for defective products. The question basically involves the nature of the obligation of the manufacturer of a product to third parties who buy the product, say, from a store which has no legal connection with the manufacturer, when the product develops a defect that causes harm to the purchaser. The law has moved in jumps through a series of key decisions in the direction of extending the manufacturer's liability in these cases. Most recently, key cases in New York and California asserted the principle that the existence of a defect need not be proved if the third party suffered harm as a consequence of putting the product to its intended use. In this case "the matter speaks for itself" and the manufacturer is held liable. This notion spread rapidly through other jurisdictions, repeating the process of verification which had a few decades before been accorded to an earlier (and weaker) extension of the law in the same area.[6] Here then was a clearcut case of judicial intervention to alter the meaning of the law and establish a new doctrine, which was quickly verified by decisions in a large number of autonomous jurisdictions. Could an economist agree that the validity of this moral principle—in the restricted area in which the courts hold it to be valid—is at least as well verified as is, say, the influence of the accelerator effect on investment?

Law and Economics

What is the relevance of all this for economics? Well, of course the aim has been to explore possibilities for getting consideration of values integrated into economic science. The process of transforming the attitudes of economists in this way seems to have three phases. The first phase requires acceptance of the idea that interpersonal comparisons can be usefully discussed in a more or less positivist way. A fair amount of attention was devoted to this proposition here, with emphasis being placed on the ubiquity of such comparisons in everyday life, the frequent existence of a central tendency in the appraisals by many people of the same comparison, and the essentially interpersonal structure of language. The role of language is perhaps most important in this argument, since a number of positivist errors have stemmed from a misconception of the nature of language.

The second phase requires acceptance of the existence currently of a process of verifying values. The case for a portion of the law as containing such a process over a quite restricted domain of values has been briefly outlined in this chapter. The key arguments here are that in this portion of the law, alternative rules of obligation are tested against the facts of human conflict situations, and that proposed solutions are tested in various jurisdictions by repeated attempts to apply them to new ranges of fact.[7]

For the third phase, what is required is the specification of a process of value verification for economics. This we will not attempt, other than to offer an obiter dictum or two on its likely properties. The key property of legal verification that is really absent in economics is the testing of alternative rules of obligation against the facts of individual situations. Acquiring experience of the situations that are being affected by policy is one of the best ways to begin the introduction of value verification. An expert evaluator must have a thorough knowledge both of the range of alternative rules of obligation that may be correct and of the range of situations to which these rules have been applied. Verification does not occur without some form of replication; the legal technique of case classification, in which testing is systematically applied to cases with marginally varying properties, should have considerable application in economics but is not the only alternative.

Suppose a system of value verification were installed and functioning in economics. What would be an optimistic appraisal of its potential? We would not be generating objective values in any absolute sense, any more than we are establishing facts to be absolutely true. Indeed, the outcome for values would be comparable to that for facts. In some cases the result of intensive effort by experts would bear fruit in consensus, in others some limits to reasonable controversy would be set, while in still others it would not be possible to make significant progress in establishing the correctness of a particular rule of obligation. That is, I believe, a worthy goal, both morally and in terms of its prospective feasibility.

16

What's Wrong with Economics II

There has probably never been a time in which neoclassical economics has not been under serious challenge. Today is no exception. But, as in the past, today there are areas of mainline economics that continue to have the power to attract good students and to arouse their enthusiasm and commitment to the development of that area. None is more successful than mathematical economics, where serious mathematics is being both developed and given economic interpretation, for the most part well within the neoclassical framework.[1] Another area that is attractive to young economists is political economics, narrowly interpreted as the neoclassical theory of collective choice. And it is still true that applied econometrics and the slightly mysterious way it pulls unexpected results out of masses of data continues to attract new enthusiasts. In all these areas, well-defined puzzles serve as the challenge, and there is little reason to suppose that interest in these puzzles will disappear in the immediate future (especially since it seems so unlikely that the puzzles will be solved in a socially useful way).

Despite the fact that these are areas that are, if anything, growing in their ability to attract young economists, it is surely true that there is a simultaneous growth in the dissatisfaction with which many economists, and particularly increasing numbers of young economists, view the performance of the profession. The rapid rise of a new organization of institutionalist economists and of the Union of Radical Political Economists are two organizational manifestations of this growing discontent, as are the comments of some of the mainline profession's leaders, quoted in earlier chapters. As has been argued, there is a good methodological basis for this malaise, and consequently the search for a new and better economics should not be restricted to marginal change through concentration on conventional puzzles.

The purpose of a methodological work is often misunderstood by practitioners of a science. The most likely response of an economist to such work is, "Well, if you can display a new and better economics in your book, you'll have something, but it's no good criticizing without offering an alternative." The position seems reasonable enough, *prima facie,* but it *is* in error, since it misunderstands the nature of the "alternative" which a methodological criticism is proposing. The appropriate response, in other words, goes like this. It is granted that a new and better economics is what we're all working toward, but that is not the minimal positive advance that can occur. The better the case for the existence of serious flaws in current practice, the better the case for an increasing number of economists to allocate a portion of their time in search of fundamentally better ways of doing economics. The creation of a new and better economics will be a joint venture.

In working on this book the author has had occasion to read quite a few social scientists' critiques of their disciplines. It was generally the case that the writer's critique was far better than his positive proposals. This is not at all surprising, for scientific work is demanding and dramatic changes in a field require a great deal of groundlaying. The methodological critique is a part of that groundlaying, serving the purpose of opening minds to the prospective success of a search over a wider territory than has been customary. But it certainly cannot do the whole job.

Nevertheless, no critique is wholly without positive implications, and that is true also of the present work. Indeed, a central argument has been that there has existed throughout the twentieth century a fairly well developed world-view that is an alternative to liberalism and whose implications for economics may be fruitfully explored. In this chapter we will try to pull together the constructive sides of previous arguments which are directly relevant for economics, not in the form of specific proposals for action, but to outline the area in which further search is needed. There is a normative appeal here, but also an attempt to keep within bounds that one might reasonably expect economists to be willing to undertake. It might be thought of as a set of general guidelines for dissidents. Even so, as a summary it is useful to begin by running quickly down the bill of particulars against economics in order to set the stage. There are five basic elements to this criticism:

1 Neoclassical economics, though it seems to possess all the basic features of a science, is also based on an ideology, which in practice restricts the range of problems considered and the procedures applied to problem-solving, and has produced criteria of scientific performance based far more on the sophistication of the intellectual input than on the quality of the output.

2 Neoclassical economics is shortsighted. The accepted procedures are at best only applicable to the consideration of marginal changes in the status quo. The formalist revolution has only served to emphasize this feature despite the Velikovskyan world of structural change which is the subject of study of economics, as of all social science.

3 Marxist economics scores substantially lower than neoclassical economics in terms of the Kuhnian tests for a science. Nevertheless, Marxism has some advantages over its brother-discipline, in particular the possession of a global search-mechanism and acceptance of the intrinsic role of values in understanding social phenomena. Contemporary Marxism has to offer, not guidance to understanding, but the opportunity to develop such understanding through resolving the fundamental conflicts among Marxist practitioners.

4 Neoclassical economics is in the peculiar position of passing all the Kuhnian tests of both a developing normal science and a science in crisis. Furthermore, this seems to have been a rather persistent feature of the discipline during most of the twentieth century. The basic problem is that fundamental anomalies do not get resolved. There were never more of them than there are today, ranging over all the central fields.

5 The current directions of social change tend to increase the significance of those parts of economics that are most heavily beset with anomalies. Most important here is the effect that increasing externalities, both positive and negative, have on the fundamental basis for evaluating economic alternatives, namely price theory.

Turning to the more positive aspects of this study, it should first be noted that methodology itself has its positive side. Essentially a significant methodological change within a science changes the nature of acceptable solutions to some of its puzzles; consequently it may also lead to the admission or exclusion of puzzles from the purview of scientists. A principal argument in Part IV was that, especially at a time of conceptual uncertainty, the appropriate verification procedure involves the interdependent bringing to bear of induction, deduction, and colligation in support of hypotheses, theories, and orientations. The scientific storyteller must try to bring the audience along with him, using whatever instruments are likely to be persuasive, while relying on his own background and that of his scientific audience, as well as the social nature of the scientific effort, to control excesses.

The sloganed version of this methodological puzzle is: Story has primacy over study. One version of it was as an explanation of the poor performance of formalist verifications: that ideology, narrow training, and professional gaming explain much of the discrepancy between the sophistication of intellectual inputs and outputs in this part of economics. Some economists believe that the basic problem is one of quality and quantity of data, and that this can be solved by a greater allocation of resources to data gathering. Others presumably still feel that the effort is successful. Hopefully, the case for the first of these explanations has been made persuasively enough to at least require some serious discussion. Some explicit application of storytelling criteria to problems, which has not been attempted here, is certainly in order.

Though economists have frequently accepted in principle the idea that values can be verified, shown to be correct or incorrect, they have never, to my knowledge, made any real effort to specify the value verification process. We have proposed a procedure which is claimed to work in practice for limited verifications of certain values applied in the law. Defense of the procedure has depended heavily on the previous arguments about the nonpositivist nature of much verification of fact. A more direct test of the thesis, which for economists can only come through attempts to develop a comparable procedure within the discipline, is very much in order. Naturally, not all values can be verified, and there will be differing degrees of verification, just as with facts. Equally naturally, the procedure is not foolproof, as the errors and prejudices of jurists through the ages can attest. But again, this issue is surely important enough to be worth a bit of the time of some competent economists. Unfortunately the interdependence among the various arguments of this work gets in the way here, for the standard positivist verification procedures make this by definition a nonpuzzle of economic science. Unless one accepts storytelling as verification, he cannot work on this value-puzzle.

In an age of uncertainty for a science, one expects the history of the field to become a more frequent topic of study as practitioners begin to question fundamentals by looking for the origins and developmental history of ideas that previously had been given unquestioned acceptance. The history of economic thought is currently a depressed area, its old puzzles largely destroyed by the impact of the formalist revolution. But Kuhn has asked some questions which serve to create new puzzles for economics which may help test the validity of some of the above methodological theses. The process of conversion to great new ideas—such as neoclassicism, Marxism, Keynesianism, and formalism, as well as to the various lesser variants—is one of these, Kuhn's thesis being that facts—particularly new facts—play a far less significant role in this process than positivists would claim, and further that this is by no means a criticism of the converts. The actual role and effects of the process of training economists is another neglected subject of considerable interest, particularly in testing the validity of the heavy role assigned here to ideology in the formation of economists and in their professional practice. The history of the most interesting period for understanding the nature of contemporary economics, the twentieth century, has been only spottily told, with the formalist revolution virtually without a historian, and the Kuhnian ideas only beginning to be felt.[2]

A special peculiarity of economics as compared with the harder natural sciences is the tendency for concepts in the former to deal simultaneously with man's inner and with his outer world. Concepts like real income, consumption, and demand have this property: on the one hand they refer to man's subjective feelings, while on the other they refer to behavior as revealed in the market place. This gives a richness of meaning to these concepts which is only distorted by behavioral tendencies to restrict their meaning to purely observable phenomena. This is also why orthodox Marxism is at once crabbed and gripping. The innerworldly situation of exploitation cannot help but grip the reader and is connoted by the language of labor value. But the physicalist interpretation of that same situation, which is the denotation of orthodox Marxist argument, remains problematic and in some respects a failure; and this while the phenomenal interpretation of suffering induced by market and capitalist relations, somehow, remains.

As the logical positivists learned and philosophers of science seem rather generally to have accepted, reductionist attempts to translate the substance of a science into a purely physicalist language are not necessarily positive in effect, for one version cannot be reduced to the other without losing some meaning, and what must be given up is likely to be crucial to understanding. Of course language *can* be clarified through effort and the two types of connotations distinguished more sharply where it is useful to do so. But the element of mixing will remain, and the phenomenal connotations will continue to cling to the behaviorist formulas, and vice versa.

Here again we have a mixing, a richness which results from the complexity of the language we use to communicate some of the richness of our experience. This richness is captured most fully and accurately in the hands of a great storyteller, imbued with the necessary techniques but keeping them in their appropriate place, immersed in the facts relevant to his story, possessed of the insight of a human who has observed his fellows with sympathy and self-recognition. Abstract languages, however "well-formed," impose on the economist a handicap he can ill afford in serious attempts to deal with social problems.[3]

Marxist economics is in a state of creative confusion. Opportunities abound for further development of this distinct economic orientation, and that is true of no other currently available orientation to economics outside the neoclassical mainline itself. However, like Spartans, Marxists have shown themselves in the past to be rather easily susceptible to corruption, too many of them displaying an insufficient independence of mind to qualify as scientists. Perhaps the most effective defense against this is to break down the longstanding bias against serious discussion of the properties of a socialist society. There are signs of beginnings in this direction as Mandel's work and, even more, Horvat's, suggest. Nevertheless, Marxism remains fundamentally a critique of existing societies, whatever their professed political persuasion. Consequently one would expect that primary progress in getting Marxism back on the scientific track will come with the development of the critical puzzles that have always been its heart.

Both neoclassical and Marxist economics have weakly developed and inherently implausible theories of man built into their structures. Straightening this out is a central problem for both fields, and in both cases the developing of a powerful theory of social influences on man is the primary desideratum. A promising line of research for both fields is the study of the determinants and consequences of patterns of behavior as captured in the notion of an identity.

"It makes all the difference in the world whether a thinker stands in personal relation to his problems, in which he sees his destiny, his need, and even his highest happiness, or can only feel and grasp them impersonally with the tentacles of cold, prying thought." These words of Nietzsche suggest the root problem from which perhaps every criticism offered in this book derives. We have institutionalized the distancing of the economist from the economees, through professional careerism, through various kinds of gaming, through the exaltation of cleverness, even through politicizing. For it is surely true that to know is to act, but to act without really knowing is not science. A bit of passion mixed with dedication to understanding how the world works: that is the formula whose embodiment in economic science we must seek.

Notes

Chapter 1

1 Thomas Kuhn, *The Structure of Scientific Revolutions* (Chicago: University of Chicago Press, 1962).

2 *The Index Of Economic Journals,* Homewood, Irwin, 9 vols., 1961–1970. This index covers all the major, and a good many minor, journals which publish a major portion of their papers in English. Of course quite a bit of neoclassical economic research is published in other languages, especially French, German, and Russian. But English is overwhelmingly the language of this particular science, and given the linguistic incompetence so typical of English and particularly American economists, the restriction makes some sense as a rough approximation.

3 Something that closely resembles some key parts of neoclassical economics is taught in the Soviet Union in the curricula of mathematical economics that during the 60's have been introduced at a number of universities. Some comments on the relation of Soviet to western neoclassical economics occur in Part II below. In the West, the American postwar dominance is probably declining. As a wild guess, the ratio of research economists at American to British academic institutions is ten to one while the U.S.–German ratio may be close to that and is rising rapidly. Development of the neo-

classical tradition is proceeding apace elsewhere on the Continent and in many parts of the Third World.

4 Allan Cartter, *An Assessment of Quality in Graduate Education* (Washington, D.C.: American Council on Education, 1966). A more recent study by Cartter was recently released. See *New York Times* (Jan. 3, 1971): 1.

5 J. K. Galbraith, after all, was quite recently elected by his peers president of the American Economic Association, an organization that surely contains a substantial majority of living economist-scientists among its 15,000 or so members. My unsubstantiated guess is that if one were to restrict the vote for such honorary offices to the narrower definition of members of the invisible college mentioned above, Galbraith would not have been selected, not because he is not respected by these economists, but rather because they do not consider him to be one, of them, to be a contributing member to the *science* of economics. It is indeed true that systematic treatment of problems of detail is not much apparent anywhere in the corpus of Galbraith's works.

6 One modest sign of convalescence is the initiation three years ago of a journal, *History of Political Economy,* devoted exclusively to scholarly publication in the subfield.

Chapter 2

1 The 1970 edition of Kuhn's book contains a chapter responding to reviewers' criticisms. One of Kuhn's favorite terms, "paradigm," came in for a good deal of criticism as being used in many different senses in the work, a criticism which Kuhn has accepted. For this reason the term is avoided, for the most part, in this work, the principal substitute concepts being world-view and Kuhn's own "network of commitments" and "puzzle."

2 Of these factors, puzzles are central to Kuhn's discussion and the others are at least mentioned by him. The treatment of stylized facts is somewhat different from Kuhn but definitely Kuhnian in spirit. The other factors are emphasized here because they are especially relevant to social science.

3 That is not to say that the puzzle is solved, in the sense that economists are now generally agreed as to which of the proposed solu-

tions is correct. The controversy has continued in various forms ever since. A summary description of the puzzle and of the earlier proposals for solution can be found in Milton Friedman, *A Theory of the Consumption Function* (Princeton: Princeton University Press, 1957), pp. 3–4.

4 The two key works around which discussion has centered are M. Krzyzaniak and R. Musgrave, *The Shifting of the Corporate Income Tax* (Baltimore: Johns Hopkins, 1963), and R. G. Gordon, "The Incidence of the Corporation Income Tax in U.S. Manufacturing, 1925–1962," *American Economic Review,* 57 (Sept., 1967): 731–758. For the most recent salvos and references to others, see the exchange between F. D. Sebold and R. G. Gordon in the *National Tax Journal,* 23 (Dec., 1970): 365–378.

5 There is plenty of fuzziness in the concept of consumption, and this has played a role in the controversy, but has not been as central and explicit a problem as in the tax shifting puzzle. Perhaps the major difference between these two puzzle-controversies is that the consumption discussion has been relatively less open-ended; that is, the participants seem to have a wider range of agreement with respect to the underlying facts and assumptions, and there has consequently been much less attempt to solve the problem by changing the puzzle.

6 For what it is worth, the author not being an econometrician, I am struck by the perfunctory nature of the defenses of applications of the strangeness rule in many well-regarded studies. Perhaps there is some awareness of the Pandora's box that taking strangeness "seriously" would open. It should be emphasized that there is no objection in principle to the use of stylized facts in general, or of the strangeness rule in particular.

7 This account is largely taken from Harry Girvetz, *The Evolution of Liberalism* (New York: Collier, 1963), Part I.

8 H. Stuart Hughes, *Consciousness and Society* (New York: Knopf, 1958). Like all such deep traditions, these, too, have their roots in the nineteenth century and before. The "generation of the 90's" is especially interesting to us because it is reacting explicitly against the social and philosophical currents that influenced the founders of neoclassical economics. Veblen and Commons are economists who come close to this group in their orientations, but neither developed a viable economic paradigm.

9 The power inherent in appointment is easily underestimated. As G.

D. H. Cole has said, "A good deal of the battle for academic freedom is actually lost before the appointments are made . . . to a substantial degree, the appearance of tranquility on the sea of English academic life is due to a very careful selection at the start." These remarks from a report on academic freedom in 1935 are quoted with tentative approval by A. W. Coats, the historian of thought, in his "Sociological Aspects of British Economic Thought (ca. 1880–1930)," *Journal of Political Economics,* 75 (1967): 706–729. Consciences are not much troubled by such practices because economics has mixed its ideology into the subject so well that the ideologically unconventional usually appear to appointment committees to be scientifically incompetent.

10 Another kind of power, the familiar one of monopoly, may be rearing its head in the profession. The major change in departmental status since the mid-60's is a strengthening of Harvard and M.I.T., the two top departments in Cartter Report terms, mainly at the expense of Chicago, Berkeley, and Stanford, the fourth-to-sixth-ranked schools. Status rankings were probably undisturbed by this, but such a heavy concentration of talent and influence in Cambridge (Yale, ranked third, is the closest major department to Cambridge), if it persists, can have a substantial effect on communication patterns within the discipline.

11 This suggests another and rather touchy point. Not only has postwar neoclassical economics been overwhelmingly an Anglo-American activity, but its new staff in the United States has been recruited equally overwhelmingly from the ranks of young white males, with a relatively high Jewish component. For what it is worth, my own impression is that this selectivity is not based on prejudice, except perhaps in the case of women. But it is true that research economics constitutes a peculiar kind of club and there are, no doubt, a variety of subtle ways by which those with the appropriate physical and cultural affinities are made relatively more welcome than others. The impact of such more-or-less unconscious practices may be felt mostly in self-selection and very little in rationing. As one goes back in time or down the status-ranking of institutions, overt and operational prejudice probably tends to increase.

Chapter 3

1 A. W. Coats, "Is there a 'Structure of Scientific Revolutions' in Economics," *Kyklos*, 22 (1969): 289–300; Axel Leijonhufvud, *On Keynesian Economics and the Economics of Keynes* (New York: Oxford University Press, 1968). However, Donald Gordon, "The Role of the History of Economic Thought in the Understanding of Modern Economic Theory," *American Economic Review*, 55 (1965, Supplement): 124, asserted that "economics has never had a major revolution; its basic maximizing model has never been replaced." This last remark is certainly correct. Taking it as an interpretation of the preceding no-revolution claim, the differences between, say, Gordon and Coats become semantic.

2 The following account of events leading up to the General Theory is largely taken from G. Mehta, *Kuhn's Historiographical Framework and the Keynesian Revolution*. Berkeley (unpublished Ph.D. thesis), 1971.

3 T. W. Hutchinson, *A Review of Economic Doctrines 1870–1929* (London: Oxford University Press, 1953), pp. 374–375.

4 Hutchinson, *op. cit.*, ch. 22–23; Mehta, *op. cit.*

5 Various attempts to keep non-neoclassical economists from British academic posts are described in A. W. Coats, "Sociological Aspects of British Economic Thought (ca. 1880–1930)," *Journal of Political Economy*, 75 (1967): 706–729.

6 The attempt to provide a microeconomic underpinning to macroeconomics is a very fashionable topic these days. See, for example, the papers in E. S. Phelps, ed., *Microeconomic Foundations of Employment and Inflation Theory* (New York: Norton, 1970). So far, the plausibility of most such micromodels remains quite dubious. For example, work on the Phillips curve in the above volume succeeded only in generating a curve that was undergoing continuous shift. George Akerlof has shown me a model in which a "stable" Phillips curve is generated by achieving balance in the adjustment rates of a pair of markets which remain generally in disequilibrium. These results are interesting, but they do not lay to rest any doubts as to the stability of asserted macroeconomic behavioral relations.

7 That is, Keynes was not responsible for the rise of big government. Causation probably runs the other way, at least in the sense that if

Keynes had not existed the needs of big government would have created him.

8 As Kenneth Arrow has put it: "But it seems to me that successively greater understanding can only come from the articulation of formal systems which incorporate more and more of our intuition and experience . . . [and then quoting Weyl] 'if the transcendental is accessible to us only through the medium of images and symbols, let the symbols at least be as distinct and unambiguous as mathematics will permit' " in "Samuelson Collected," *Journal of Political Economy*, 75 (1967): 737.

9 Institutionalist humor tended to be based on allusive incongruities, such as an unexpected application of a traditional aphorism. Formalist humor tends to be based on puzzle incongruities, such as a meaning shift based on an unexpected word interchange. The following one-liner contains elements of both these styles and, appropriately enough, was told by a modernized institutionalist: To paraphrase Oscar Wilde, a Soviet planner is a person who knows the value of everything, the price of nothing.

10 Sir John Clapham, "Of Empty Economic Boxes," *Economic Journal*, 32 (1922): 305–314.

11 For example, the net productivity controversy, or the interpretation of the integrability conditions for marginal utility functions.

12 Some might wish to object that growth theory has developed a variety of fundamental conceptual novelties since 1950—for example, the Turnpike and Golden Age theorems. The author is no expert in this area but finds these developments essentially uninteresting because the quite longrun stability of parameters and functional forms they require are so wildly inappropriate, and most particularly inappropriate to dynamic analysis. They are based more on theorem-seeking assumptions than on truth-seeking ones.

13 This argument is my version of the outcome of a sunny, relaxed, and not wholly serious lunchtime discussion on the terrace at Berkeley a few years ago. The existence of an age-gap was perhaps proposed by Bernard Saffran, and this hypothesis was immediately subjected to, and passed, a rigorous name-dropping test. The most popular explanations of the gap were, if I recall, the narrow range of Ph.D.-producing schools that were staffed in the new orientation twenty years ago, and the paucity at that time of first-rate (meaning mathematically acute) minds coming into economics.

14 Arrow, *op. cit.*, 734, 734n.

15 Paul Feyerabend, a quantum physicist turned philosopher, has called for permanent revolution (in the Kuhnian sense of open-ended search and questioning of fundamentals) for quantum physics, though he stops short of saying that is what they've got. See "Problems of Microphysics" in S. Morgenbesser, ed., *Philosophy of Science Today* (New York: Basic Books, 1967).

16 His best known works are *Worlds in Collision* (New York: Doubleday, 1950) and *Earth in Upheaval* (New York: Doubleday, 1955).

Chapter 4

1 When labor is treated as the scarce input, an input-output model's price system is a labor-value theory, as Leontief pointed out in his prewar book on the subject. In contemporary planning applications it is by no means uncommon to treat labor as the scarce input. In constructing an index of Soviet production some years ago Donald Hodgman assumed that value added was adequately approximated by wage bills for the purpose of weighting (that is, valuing) production in various industries. These uses can be taken as evidence that labor value is plausible as a stylized fact even within the neoclassical fold.

2 Marx's writings on France exhibit this aspect of his theory most clearly, especially the *Class Struggle in France* and the *Eighteenth Brumaire of Louis Napoleon.*

3 Nevertheless, the specification of the Marxian definition of class for the contemporary world remains unclear. See ch. 5, n. 8.

4 The imperialism discussion acquired much of its structure from John A. Hobson's book on the subject. Hobson was neither neoclassical nor Marxist, but in the development of economics his influence was primarily on Marxism, since only it could handle such large issues.

5 One might want to include someone like V. V. Novozhilov, who wrote several papers attempting to merge elements of neoclassical price theory with Marxian value notions. But the clear intent of his work was precisely what the Soviet ideologs feared: to provide a basis for doing neoclassical economics under a nominally Marxian rubric. No attempt was made to operate within the framework of Marxian puzzles as these were described above.

Chapter 5

1 This view is shared by Ernest Mandel; see his *Marxist Economic Theory*, vol. 2 (New York: Monthly Review, 1968), p. 723.

2 This feeling is enhanced for the reader by the organization given by Nicholas Spulber to his very useful collection of translations from this period, *Foundations of the Soviet Strategy for Economic Development* (Bloomington: Indiana University Press, 1964).

3 Paul Baran, *The Political Economy of Growth* (New York: Monthly Review, 1957); Ernest Mandel, *op. cit.* (the original French version appeared in 1962); Branko Horvat, *Toward a Theory of Planned Economy* (Belgrade: YIER, 1964) (the original Serbo-Croatian version appeared in 1961); and Herbert Marcuse, *One Dimensional Man* (Boston: Beacon, 1964).

4 Horvat studied for a time at the University of Manchester, and he is also the most nearly neoclassical of the four.

5 L. V. Kantorovich, *Economic Calculation of the Best Use of Resources* (Russian) (Moscow, 1960). The author's vision of a price-based Soviet socialist economy occurs at pp. 166–169, 232–239.

6 Stojanović lists a number of "important" writers during this period, but none of them is an economist.

7 "Marxism and Socialism Now," *New York Review of Books*, 16, No. 12 (July 1, 1971): 16.

8 A number of central problems in Marxism are worth further discussion, but only two will be mentioned here to lend substance to the claim that there is indeed a crisis. First, the major failure of internationalism, a major tenet of classical Marxism. Today all Communist parties with influence internationally, and particularly in revolutionary times, use nationalism to the full as a supplement to the typically rather weak socialist solidarity. The history of the twentieth century has shown decisively enough that nationalism lends itself to the support of postrevolutionary policy issues, with disastrous consequences both domestically and internationally. Second, there is no real agreement as to what a class is in the modern world. For example, it is not at all clear that in developed countries, and particularly the United States, the traditional blue-collar working class has many of the features of the exploited workers of classical Marxism, but most Marxists continue to be-

have as if this were true, presumably in part because their base of political support lies there. Again, the ingredients of a major crisis in Marxist economic thought are everywhere at hand.

Chapter 6

1 The writer is informed that western policy-oriented behavioral works in both economics and political science are a staple of instruction in the Hungarian Higher Party School's curriculum. How to stay in power while recognizing only some of the claims of established interests is a question of central interest to most of the world's establishments. A Marxist might agree that the most detailed and useful answers to that question are most likely to come from those parts of the world in which experience in answering it has the longest continuous tradition.

2 There is some indication in his text (*op. cit.,* 167–168) that Kuhn believes that the six tests of a normal science, paraphrased in the present work on pp. 5–7, are both necessary and sufficient for the existence of a science. Probably most philosophers of science would accept their necessity, but sufficiency certainly remains controversial. Do the tests really suffice to exclude say theology and astrology? We can hardly apply the tests to such areas here, though I hazard the speculation that both those fields fail the invisible college test. But if the analysis in the text is correct, passing the tests has not sufficed to make neoclassical economics an acceptably performing science. What appears to be required to obtain sufficiency is some appraisal of the nature of the aspects of nature under study by the particular discipline and of the appropriateness of the discipline's procedures to the study of such phenomena. The lesson of economics is that it is not always enough that, for example, practitioners are in substantial agreement as to the properties of acceptable puzzles and their solutions to insure that a science is seriously engaged in the attempt to understand the relevant natural phenomena. Perhaps one might want to argue that economics includes Marxism, and that this expanded notion of the discipline fails the invisible college test, because of the lack of cohesion and common background of its members. In that case, clearly twentieth-century social sciences are all nonsciences in the Kuhnian sense, and one would want to add the additional suffi-

ciency test in order to distinguish things like economics from things like theology.

Chapter 7

1 C. West Churchman, *Challenge to Reason* (New York: McGraw-Hill, 1968), p. 140.

2 Robert C. Carson, *Interaction Concepts of Personality* (Chicago: Aldine, 1969), p. 16.

3 For surveys, with references, of personality theory and developmental psychology, see respectively L. J. Bischof, *Interpreting Personality Theories* (New York: Harper & Row, 1964), and G. M. Gilbert, *Personality Dynamics, A Biosocial Approach* (New York: Harper & Row, 1970). Surveys of theories of personality change can be found in P. Worchel and D. Byrne, eds., *Personality Change* (New York: John Wiley, 1964).

4 Leon Festinger and J. M. Carlsmith, "Cognitive Consequences of Forced Compliance," *Journal of Abnormal Social Psychology,* 58 (1959): 203–210. This experiment forms the basis of a large literature, which is surveyed and discussed in Robert P. Abelson et al., eds., *Theories of Cognitive Consistency: A Sourcebook* (Chicago: Rand McNally, 1968), especially chs. 4, 81–84. The results described in the text are from a later and revised version of the experiment reported in J. M. Carlsmith et al., "Studies in Forced Compliance: I," *Journal of Personality and Social Psychology,* 4 (1966): 1–13. There is, of course, a good deal more to the theory than the proposition or two stated in the text.

5 N. R. Hanson has frequently made use of such Gestaltist figures in interpreting scientific behavior, for example in his "Observation and Interpretation," in S. Morgenbesser, ed., *Philosophy of Science Today* (New York: Basic Books, 1967), pp. 91–95.

6 J. S. Bruner and L. Postman, "On the Perception of Incongruity: A Paradigm," *Journal of Personality,* 18 (1949): 206–223. Kuhn makes very effective use of this experiment in his work, *op. cit.,* 62–64.

7 In this connection, see Janet G. Moore, *Many Ways of Seeing* (Cleveland: World, 1968), p. 118.

8 Milovan Djilas, *The Unperfect Society* (New York: Harcourt, Brace and World, 1969), p. 26.

9 A brief interpretative account of this process and its consequences in the Society of Jesus, the interwar U.S. Navy officer corps, and the Soviet Communist party, occurs in B. Ward, *The Socialist Economy, A Study of Organizational Alternatives* (New York: Random House, 1967), ch. 5 *et seq.*

Chapter 8

1 H. G. Grubel and A. D. Scott, in "The Characteristics of Foreigners in the U. S. Economics Profession," *American Economics Review,* 57 (1967): 131–145, have shown the high incidence of foreign-born and foreign-educated economists relative to the distribution of these traits in the population of the United States. We are more interested here in the incidence of foreign-educated leading scholars and, impressionistically, it is still higher.

2 For a detailed survey of French Marxism that supports this appraisal, see George Lichtheim, *Marxism in Modern France* (New York: Columbia, 1966), chs. 3–5.

3 *MT* (*Mechanical Translation and Computational Linguistics*), Chicago, the major journal of machine translation research, ceased publication in 1968. Some of the last articles it published showed these translation techniques failing comparison tests on scientific texts with even relatively naïve "manual" translation procedures. See David B. Orr and V. H. Small, "Comprehensibility of Machine-Aided Translations of Russian Scientific Documents," *MT,* 10 (1967): 1–10. For a glance at the modesty with which an optimist's claims are presented these days see A. Ljudskanov, "Is the Generally Accepted Strategy of Machine-Translation Research Optimal?", *MT,* 11 (1968): 14–21.

4 In the apt phrase of Sidney Winter, "Science as a Consensus System: Five Fragments and a Dialogue," RAND, D-17524-PR (1968).

5 Progress is perhaps the wrong word to use in discussing philosophy, which is the field of permanent revolution *par excellence.* At any rate, this has been the program of language philosophers such as Austin, Wisdom, and Ryle. A succinct account of this work, with references, can be found in John Passmore, *A Hundred Years of Philosophy,* rev. ed. (New York: Basic Books, 1966), ch. 18.

6 Chomsky's own most accessible account of this idea is in his

Cartesian Linguistics (New York: Harper & Row, 1966). Chomsky's work in this area is very nicely appraised by Ved Mehta in *The New Yorker* (May 8, 1971), 44–87.

7 Ludwig Wittgenstein, *Philosophical Investigations* (New York: Macmillan, 1953).

8 Perhaps the most accessible introduction to the existential idea of man consists of the first three essays in Rollo May et al., eds., *Existence* (New York: Basic Books, 1958), currently available in a Clarion paperback.

Chapter 9

1 The change in tastes mentioned here does not contradict previous remarks on the subject. For the change here is exogenous, unanalyzed, a *deus ex machina* rather than the subject of serious study.

2 Again the bias in such accounts as do exist is inherent in the theory and not the conscious product of the theorist. The theories glibly assume away most of the distinguishing properties of information such as its uniqueness and nonappropriability. For these issues, see Kenneth Arrow's profound and destructive piece, "Classificatory Notes on the Production and Transmission of Technological Knowledge," *American Economics Review,* 59 (May, 1969): 29–35. Treatments of information to date are for the most part good examples of the distortions that theorem-seeking investigation can produce.

3 Despite the excesses detailed in L. L. Thomas, *The Linguistic Theories of N. Marr,* Berkeley (unpublished Ph.D. thesis), 1954. The significance of the Marr controversy for Marxism is discussed in Alvin Gouldner, *The Coming Crisis of Western Sociology* (New York: Basic Books, 1970). Gouldner's appraisal of sociology somewhat parallels the present appraisal of economics, with "Parsonsianism" playing the role of neoclassical economics.

4 Frank Knight, *Ethics of Competition* (New York: Harper & Row, 1935), p. 78.

5 Alfred Marshall's great work, *Principles of Economics,* 8th ed. (London: Macmillan, 1920) contains striking support for the centrality of induced taste-change (Book III, ch. 2 and 3) and makes very modest claims for the consumer analysis that now dominates the

textbooks. For a contemporary but unconventional account of taste-change by an economist well-versed in neoclassical theory, see E. J. Mishan, *The Costs of Economic Growth* (London: Staples, 1967).

6 A typically indifferent reaction to research on the topic, coming just after an explicit recognition of the fundamental importance of the issue, is the following: "No research that I know of has detected a wrinkle in aggregate consumer spending behavior that can be traced to the beginning of television. Perhaps no one has tried. Pending some evidence, I am not inclined to take this popular doctrine very seriously" (Robert M. Solow, "The New Industrial State or Son of Affluence," *Public Interest,* 9 (Fall, 1967): 105. As was suggested above, within the neoclassical framework this attitude is wholly justified. The present theory is far too weak to carry the additional burden of preference change. But this leaves ideology in the driver's seat, discouraging the search for a framework that would get at the issue, in contradiction to a later statement by the same economist: "But I would also assert that there is far less ideology wrapped up in academic economics in the United States than a man from Cambridge, England, can possibly realize." In "The Truth Further Refined: A Comment on Marris," *op. cit.,* 11 (Spring, 1968): 52.

7 Perhaps most important is the failure to develop a good library and retrieval system for photographs. Even so intensive a user as *Life* apparently has no satisfactory answer to this problem. William Garnett's proposal to develop such a system around a file of current-history (broadly conceived) photographs, partly developed by the library itself, is one of those great ideas presently languishing for lack of support.

8 David C. McClelland, *The Achieving Society* (Princeton: Van Nostrand, 1961); D. C. McClelland and D. G. Winter, *Motivating Economic Achievement* (New York: Free Press, 1969). For the attitude toward business risk of the high-achievement-need subject, see the latter volume, pp. 51, 55, 338–339.

Chapter 10

1 The reader may object that GNP is a descriptive, value-neutral concept, so that one may perfectly consistently maintain both that

GNP has risen and that that is a bad thing. Quite so, but words are deeds, GNP was constructed both by theorists and statisticians as an aggregative measure of welfare, and no serious attempt has been made to fit income distribution—or even good direct measures of poverty—into typical macroeconomic models. Public policy discussions about economic performance *do* center around the GNP concept, with the twin additions of the inflation rate and the rate of unemployment, the latter two having a somewhat indirect relation to distributive-poverty questions. And there is a high degree of overlap between those who have doubts about growth as a desideratum and those who object to the GNP concept. If GNP becomes generally thought to be a poor measure of performance, it will probably cease to be measured.

2 Wassily Leontief, "Theoretical Assumptions and Nonobserved Facts," *American Economics Review,* 61 (March, 1971): 1.

3 Ernest Nagel, *Principles of the Theory of Probability* (Chicago: University of Chicago Press, 1939), p. 6.

4 The idea is described in Luce and Raiffa, *op. cit.,* pp. 282–284.

5 The parable poses in an interesting way the fundamental question as to who should set the dial, who should prescribe the "attitude" of nature. Leaving this issue of principle aside, it should be noted that in the situation of the typical econometric problem, which involves data which are poor both in quantity and quality by hard-science standards, there is not a discernible shift parameter to serve as the Hurwicz dial. Instead, its setting is fixed indirectly, probably for the most part by the choice of stylized facts, including the so-called maintained hypotheses which are required by the particular statistical model chosen. Consequently a study of the same problem by an investigator with a different view of nature's benevolence will probably differ in a *number* of respects from the original study. The world-view choice is thus screened from the reader's view by being mixed in with several partly substantive choices in the specification of the problem.

Chapter 11

1 J. S. Mill, *A System of Logic* (London: Parker, 1843); W. S. Jevons, *The Principles of Science* (London: Macmillan, 1874); J. M.

Keynes, *A Treatise on Probability* (London: Macmillan, 1921); Roy F. Harrod, *Foundations of Inductive Logic* (New York: Harcourt, Brace, 1957).

2 Karl R. Popper, *The Logic of Scientific Discovery* (London: Hutchinson, 1958) (German original, 1934); Harold Jeffreys, *Theory of Probability* (London: Oxford, 1939); L. J. Savage, *The Foundations of Statistics* (New York: John Wiley, 1954).

3 Max Black, "The Justification of Induction," in S. Morgenbesser, *op. cit.*, p. 200.

4 R. B. Braithwaite, *Scientific Explanation* (New York: Harper & Row, 1960), p. 255.

5 Popper himself was not a formal probabilist; that is, he did not believe that the considerations that are usually relevant in determining the relative corroboration of hypotheses lent themselves to numerical estimation. *Op. cit.*, 268. Popper's account of corroboration (ch. 10) comes pretty close to the views expressed here.

6 Michael Polanyi, *Personal Knowledge* (Chicago: University of Chicago Press, 1958); N. R. Hanson, *Patterns of Discovery* (Cambridge: Cambridge University Press, 1958); Thomas Kuhn, *op. cit.*

7 William Whewell, *The Philosophy of the Inductive Sciences* (London: Parker, 1847), book XI, especially ch. 4.

8 W. V. Quine, *From a Logical Point of View* (Cambridge: Harvard University Press, 1964), p. 43; quoted in Winter, *op. cit.*

9 Andreas G. Papandreou, *Economics as a Science* (Philadelphia, Lippincott, 1958), showed how this works in the comparative static analysis widely used in economics.

10 This point bears on the role that the problem-oriented team has played in social-science research in recent years. A team of behavioralists from several disciplines can often work well together because they have already acquired the basis for a common language as a result of their behavioral orientation. It is not so difficult to get a behavioral political scientist to understand a new concept from economics because both share a common background of orientations and maintained hypotheses. But of course this commonalty is bought at the price of an intellectual search by the team which is restricted by the narrow perspectives of behaviorism. The dilemma is that broadening the representation of conceptual orientations on the team creates fundamental language problems whose solution must precede a genuine team effort.

11 Popper—at least the Popper of *The Logic* . . .—would accept most of this. The problem is that economists have not kept up with the theory of verification, or do not really want to take this problem seriously.

12 In practice specification of models depends crucially on deciding that certain variables are *not* dependent on certain others. But that does not invalidate the basic message of the Fundamental Preconception, which has to do with openendedness, as noted in the text.

13 In principle these ignored variables all make their appearance in the error term of each equation. But in practice a serious attempt is just not made to defend the assumptions necessary to this approach, and for a very simple reason: nobody would be persuaded.

14 Naturally this does not imply that econometrics is useless. Its proper place in the scheme of verification is suggested in the next chapter.

15 Mark Blaug, *Economic Theory in Retrospect,* rev. ed. (Homewood: Irwin, 1968), pp. 667, 669. Blaug devotes a section to "The Limitations of the Falsifiability Criterion in Economics," pp. 671–675.

16 "But when asked to lecture on 'What Economists Know,' he does not at any point refer to the allocation of resources through the price system. . . . This omission is no accident; a careful examination of the papers both on theory and on policy yields only the most oblique suggestions that neoclassical price theory is descriptive of the real world. . . . After all, the descriptive propositions of neoclassical price theory are only hypothetical propositions . . . ; yet the elaboration of such propositions is clearly a revealed preference of Samuelson's. . . . But after referring the formation of social policy to an all-embracing social welfare function, the discussion stops." *Op. cit.,* pp. 733, 736. It should be emphasized that Arrow is really directing these remarks at "best-practice" economics, as exemplified by Samuelson. "Samuelson is one of the greatest economic theorists of all time . . . the last two somewhat critical sections . . . have been used as a mirror for all of us": pp. 735, 737.

17 J. M. Keynes, "Fluctuations in Net Investment in the United States," *Economic Journal,* 46 (1936): 540–547. Colin Clark estimated the multiplier for the United Kingdom in "Determination of the Multiplier From National Income Statistics," *Economic Journal,* 48 (1938): 435–448, in a much more substantial effort based on

somewhat shaky data and assumptions, but this paper does not seem to have been widely accepted.

18 Lorie Tarshis, "Changes in Real and Money Wages," *Economic Journal,* 49 (1939): 150–154.

19 Jan Tinbergen, *An Econometric Approach to Business Cycle Problems* (Paris: Hermann, 1939). He estimated impact multipliers which were not directly of policy relevance, and his study does not seem to have gotten into the mainstream discussion of Keynesianism until quite late.

20 By Arthur S. Goldberger in a paper read at the 1958 meetings of the Econometric Society. The results were published in his *Impact Multipliers and Dynamic Properties of the Klein-Goldberger Model* (Amsterdam: North-Holland, 1959).

Chapter 12

1 Sidney Schoeffler's *The Failures of Economics: A Diagnostic Study* (Cambridge: Harvard University Press, 1955), contains many of the same criticisms of the verification process as practiced by economists that have been made in the present work. He places particular emphasis on the role of structural change and of what we have called the Fundamental Preconception in reducing the reliability of formalist verification. Schoeffler's attitude toward storytelling is somewhat ambiguous: he calls stories "makeshifts" but also says that "they are of very considerable practical usefulness" (pp. 150–153) and suggests the Council's Report as a good example of the genre. Schoeffler's work preceded the period of massive application of formalist techniques to verification, and the apparent vindication of his predictions regarding reliability suggests that maybe methodology *does* have something useful to say to economics. His "General Recommendations" (pp. 162–164) do not coincide with those of the present work, but his second recommendation seems roughly equivalent to putting storytelling, as characterized in the present chapter, into the central place in much of economics.

2 Marshall on want creation is a good example. Compare the very strong statements in Book III, ch. 2 and 3, of his *Principles,* with a modern text.

Chapter 13

1 Point 5 probably contains the first statement on the list that positivist economists might claim not to believe. However, it does seem to be an implicit belief which may at least emerge in unguarded moments—for example, "Efficiency is a purely technological concept, having to do only with production," following a more acceptable formula on the preceding page. Robert Dorfman, Paul Samuelson and Robert Solow, *Linear Programming and Economic Analysis* (New York: McGraw-Hill, 1948), pp. 392, 391.

2 In his review of Samuelson's collected works, Arrow has captured neatly the neoclassical mood in this borderline area: "I suspect that the partial and limited nature of Samuelson's investigations in the foundations of welfare economics owes a great deal to his profound sense that such investigation would lead to deep and paradoxical levels of thought and feeling, where the mind and the judgment chase their own tails." "Samuelson Collected," *Journal of Political Economy,* 75 (1967): 736–737.

3 Already noted was the countertendency for the social structure to adapt to the world-views dominant in the society.

4 Optimality theorems about socialism are lost too, but they deal with a very peculiar kind of socialism in which most socialist principles are already excluded by assumption. About the only feature of socialism retained in these models is nationalization of industry; they might as well be called models of efficient fascism.

5 Various dodges are employed to separate out for the economist's domain problems in which interpersonal comparisons are avoided —for example, by assigning to individuals both "tastes" and "values," the former being the ones of principal interest to economists. The Rube Goldberg nature of some of the distinctions that are made is a testimonial to the strength with which the liberal positivist orientation dominates neoclassical economics.

6 Frank Knight, like Marshall, recognizes the interdependence but then drops it from economic science. See the essays, "Economic Psychology and the Value Problem" and "Marginal Utility Economics" in his *Ethics of Competition, op. cit.*

7 C. West Churchman, "On the Intercomparison of Utilities," in Sherman R. Krupp, ed., *The Structure of Economic Science* (Englewood

Cliffs: Prentice-Hall, 1966), pp. 247–248. The original story appears in R. Duncan Luce and H. Raiffa, *Games and Decisions* (New York: John Wiley, 1957), pp. 33–34.

Chapter 14

1 John Searle, "How to Derive 'Ought' from 'Is'," *Philosophical Review,* 73 (1964): 43–58; Max Black, "The Gap between 'Is' and 'Should'," *op. cit.,* 165–181.

2 John R. Searle, *Speech Acts* (London: Cambridge University Press, 1969).

3 The argument is published as Louis D. Brandeis, *Curt Muller in Error, Plaintiff vs. State of Oregon,* Supreme Court of the United States, October Term, 1907, no. 107 (Boston, 1908).

4 Amartya K. Sen, *Collective Choice and Social Welfare* (San Francisco: Holden-Day, 1970), p. 57, comments on the frequency of this problem in the welfare economics literature.

5 See ch. 13, n. 1.

6 The difficulties with the concept of national income have been the subject of much discussion. See Paul Samuelson, "Evaluation of Real National Income," *Collected Scientific Papers of Paul A. Samuelson* (Cambridge: M.I.T. Press, 1966), pp. 1044–1072. More recently, "ecological" concepts have been proposed, for example by William Nordhaus and James Tobin, "Is Growth Obsolete," New Haven, 1970 (mimeo) though their discussion of values lies well within neoclassical traditions.

7 R. M. Hare, *The Language of Morals* (Oxford: Clarendon, 1952); and especially in his *Freedom and Reason* (Oxford, 1963).

8 Sen, *op. cit.,* 197.

9 P. H. Nowell-Smith appraises this issue in his *Ethics* (Harmondsworth: Penguin, 1954), chs. 15, 21.

10 Kenneth E. Boulding, *The Image* (Ann Arbor: University of Michigan Press, 1956), p. 173.

11 Maurice Cornforth, *Marxism and the Linguistic Philosophy* (New York: International Publishers, 1967), p. 293.

12 Joseph Fletcher, *Situation Ethics, The New Morality* (Philadelphia: Westminster, 1966).

Chapter 15

1 A major controversy has been raging among lawyers for many years over the question as to whether a legal system existed under the Nazis in Germany, when frequent political interventions into the legal process occurred. The major recent protagonists have been H. L. A. Hart and Lon L. Fuller; see their respective books, *Concept of Law* (Oxford: Clarendon, 1961) and *Morality of Law* (New Haven: Yale University Press, 1964), for discussion and references. There is a genuine dilemma here, known in socialist literature as the Red versus expert problem. Professionals exist within a society on which they have some effect; consequently a right of society to constrain professional behavior in certain respects seems quite justifiable. All social science is beset with this problem; perhaps all science is, as the history of the *Bulletin of the Atomic Scientists* suggests.

2 The legislative threat of a new statute can serve as a constraint on judicial decisions. To some extent this may be thought of as outside intervention disrupting collegial judgment. It is also partly a matter of judicial interpretation, this time of expected statutes.

3 Strongly convergent properties of Continental and Anglo-American law in a number of areas in the twentieth century are discussed in W. Friedmann, *Law in a Changing Society,* (Berkeley: University of California Press, 1959). This does not imply that all legal systems have the same scientific components.

4 NLRB v. Hearst Publications, Inc.; 322 US 111 (1944).

5 For example, Judge Hand ruled that a seagoing tug owner was liable for storm damages to cargo because he did not carry a radio, on which he could have obtained weather reports, even though it was not customary for tugs to be radio equipped at the time. For selections from Hand's rulings in these cases, see Hershel Shanks, ed., *The Art and Craft of Judging: The Decisions of Judge Learned Hand* (New York: Macmillan, 1968).

6 The history of product liability is briefly reviewed in Robert E. Keeton, *Venturing to do Justice,* (Cambridge: Harvard University Press, 1969).

7 The argument that values are verified within the legal system is perfectly consistent with the argument that that system contains fundamental flaws as a moral science. The most obvious of these

flaws is that throughout its Anglo-American history the legal system has been controlled by an élite and administered in the interests of socially and politically dominant groups. This is perhaps most clearly seen in criminal law, and permeates all cross-class conflict situations in which the law is involved. However, large segments of tort law relate to infra-élite conflict and so largely escape this sort of taint. It is in such areas, I believe, that the achievements and possibilities of law as a moral science emerge most clearly.

Chapter 16

1 A partial exception to the no-normative-discussion rule occurs in a borderline area of economics: bargaining theory or the study of fair games. An attempt is made there to devise formal rules of allocation which meet some defended criteria of fairness. So far the level of abstraction both of the characterization of the allocative problem and of the fairness criteria is too high to permit any practical application, but future applicability is by no means excluded, and this theory has some interesting parts. For a succinct survey and appraisal of literature and results see D. G. Decavèle, *An Essentially Non-probabilistic Approach to Bargaining Theory,* Berkeley (unpublished Ph.D. thesis) 1971.

2 The principal exception to the last claim is A. W. Coats, some of whose work has been cited *supra.*

3 One remembers at this point the related remarks of Marshall on "long trains of deductive reasoning" (*Principles, op. cit.,* p. 781), and Keynes on the defects of "symbolic pseudomathematical methods of formalising a system of economic analysis" (*General Theory,* pp. 297–298). Writers keep coming back to them, perhaps because there is some fire beneath the smoke.

Index